HOW TO WIN
YOUR CASE IN
SMALL CLAIMS
COURT WITHOUT A
LAWYER

By Charlie Mann

How to Win Your Case In Small Claims Court Without a Lawyer

Copyright © 2009 by Atlantic Publishing Group, Inc.
1405 SW 6th Ave. • Ocala, Florida 34471 • 800-814-1132 • 352-622-1875—Fax
Web site: www.atlantic-pub.com • E-mail: sales@atlantic-pub.com
SAN Number: 268-1250

ISBN-13: 978-1-60138-306-8   ISBN-10: 1-60138-306-1

Library of Congress Cataloging-in-Publication Data

Mann, Charlie, 1944-
  How to win your case in small claims court without a lawyer
/ by Charlie Mann.
      p. cm.
  Includes bibliographical references and index.
  ISBN-13: 978-1-60138-306-8 (alk. paper)
  ISBN-10: 1-60138-306-1 (alk. paper)
  1. Small claims courts — United States — Popular works. 2. Pro se representation — United States Popular works. 3. Actions and defenses — United States — Popular works. 4. Trial practice — United States — Popular works. I. Title.

  KF8769.M36.2009
  347.73'28--dc22
                          2008038275

Printed in the United States

Printed on Recycled Paper

PROJECT MANAGER: Melissa Peterson • mpeterson@atlantic-pub.com
INTERIOR DESIGN: Nicole Deck • ndeck@atlantic-pub.com
BACK COVER DESIGN: Nicole Orr • norr@atlantic-pub.com
COVER DESIGN: Meg Buchner • mbuchner@atlantic-pub.com

We recently lost our beloved pet "Bear," who was not only our best and dearest friend but also the "Vice President of Sunshine" here at Atlantic Publishing. He did not receive a salary but worked tirelessly 24 hours a day to please his parents. Bear was a rescue dog that turned around and showered myself, my wife Sherri, his grandparents Jean, Bob, and Nancy and every person and animal he met (maybe not rabbits) with friendship and love. He made a lot of people smile every day.

We wanted you to know that a portion of the profits of this book will be donated to The Humane Society of the United States. *–Douglas & Sherri Brown*

The human-animal bond is as old as human history. We cherish our animal companions for their unconditional affection and acceptance. We feel a thrill when we glimpse wild creatures in their natural habitat or in our own backyard.

Unfortunately, the human-animal bond has at times been weakened. Humans have exploited some animal species to the point of extinction.

The Humane Society of the United States makes a difference in the lives of animals here at home and worldwide. The HSUS is dedicated to creating a world where our relationship with animals is guided by compassion. We seek a truly humane society in which animals are respected for their intrinsic value, and where the human-animal bond is strong.

Want to help animals? We have plenty of suggestions. Adopt a pet from a local shelter, join The Humane Society and be a part of our work to help companion animals and wildlife. You will be funding our educational, legislative, investigative, and outreach projects in the U.S. and across the globe.

Or perhaps you'd like to make a memorial donation in honor of a pet, friend, or relative? You can through our Kindred Spirits program. And if you'd like to contribute in a more structured way, our Planned Giving Office has suggestions about estate planning, annuities, and even gifts of stock that avoid capital gains taxes.

Maybe you have land that you would like to preserve as a lasting habitat for wildlife. Our Wildlife Land Trust can help you. Perhaps the land you want to share is a backyard—that's enough. Our Urban Wildlife Sanctuary Program will show you how to create a habitat for your wild neighbors.

So you see, it's easy to help animals. And The HSUS is here to help.

THE HUMANE SOCIETY
OF THE UNITED STATES.

2100 L Street NW • Washington, DC 20037 • 202-452-1100

www.hsus.org

Dedication

To my wife, Phyllis
Your support and love
are my
inspiration and motivation

-and-

In loving memory of my
brother, David, and sister, Paula

Table Of Contents

DEDICATION..4

TABLE OF CONTENTS 5

PREFACE... 13

CHAPTER 1: A WORLD FULL OF DISPUTES.......... 17

Who Can You Sue?..17

What Kinds of Lawsuits Are Possible? 18

The Rule of Law...19

The Psychology of Litigation..19

The Judgment-Proof Defendant.......................................20

The Need for This Book...20

**CHAPTER 2: PREPARING FOR
SMALL CLAIMS COURT**.................................... 23

Does Your Loss Fit the Limits of Small Claims Court? 31

Shopping for the Best Forum 33

Getting State Forms and Filing with the Court 33

Summary...35

CHAPTER 3: DO YOU HAVE A GOOD CASE?........37

Getting Help in Analyzing Your Case Details...............................39

Whom to Sue...42

Steps to the Court Clerk's Door..42

Estimating Your Loss Plus Costs...47

Making Your Case Fit State Limits 52

Free Resources for Help...53

Summary...55

CHAPTER 4: PREPARING FOR
WHAT CAN GO WRONG 57

Defendant's Rights 57

Summary...60

CHAPTER 5: SPECIAL SOLUTIONS
FOR SPECIFIC CASES..61

Types of Cases Allowed in Small Claims Court 61

Special Courts 81

CHAPTER 6: BANKRUPTCY (341A HEARING, REPRESENTATION FOR YOURSELF) 83

Off-limit Cases 83

Summary 85

CHAPTER 7: GETTING ORGANIZED FOR SMALL CLAIMS COURT 87

Where Is the Court? 87

Who Is the Defendant? 89

The Court Paperwork 89

Finding Evidence, Experts, and Witnesses 97

Do You Need an Attorney's Review? 98

Hard-to-Find Evidence or Witnesses 98

Creating an Organizer for the Trial Date 99

Visiting the Court Before Your Trial 101

Summary 101

CHAPTER 8: POTENTIAL PROBLEMS BEFORE THE COURT DATE 103

Where Is the Defendant? 103

Postal or Private Mailbox Holder 103

Issues Related to Service of the Defendant............................107

Who Should Be Served? 109

Defendant's Right to an Attorney..................................110

Defendant Strategies to Avoid Going to Trial   110

State-Required Alternatives to Trial 113

Summary..113

CHAPTER 9: PREPARING FOR YOUR DAY IN COURT........ 115

Formal Discovery 115

Selecting the Jury 117

The Opening statement 119

Witness Testimony 122

Cross-examination..124

Presenting Evidence...126

The Closing Argument..127

Summary..128

CHAPTER 10: THE NEED, SELECTION, AND USE OF AN EXPERT WITNESS 129

Do YOU Need an Expert Witness? 129

Can You Afford an Expert Witness?...................................130

Using The Internet to Locate and Obtain Written Expert Opinions..134

Court-Appointed Expert Witnesses 134

Alternatives to an Expert Witness 135

Testimony by Letter or Other Means..................................135

Choosing the Right Expert...138

Summary...140

CHAPTER 11: THE TRIAL DAY............................ 141

Present Your Case to the Judge 141

Keep the Presentation Logical..145

Be Prepared for Any Unexpected Event 146

Try to Follow Your Plan...147

Presentation of an Expert witness 149

The Judgment 149

Summary...150

CHAPTER 12: ALL IS NOT LOST
IF YOUR OPPONENT WINS.................................. 151

If You Lose, Fight Back...151

Appeal or Second Trial..155

Double Jeopardy 156

Summary..156

CHAPTER 13: APPROACHING THE DEFENDANT FOR PAYMENT 157

Try Collecting Right Away 157

Compromise to Get Quick Payment 164

Summary..165

CHAPTER 14: FINDING ASSETS 167

Having the Court Help You Collect 167

Summary..173

CHAPTER 15: WINNING IS ONLY HALF THE BATTLE.................................... 175

Necessary Collection Paperwork......................................175

Collection May Be the Most Difficult Part 178

Summary..187

CHAPTER 16: THE COLLECTION OF THEJUDGMENT 189

Collection Techniques That Work.....................................191

Is It Better to Pay Someone toCollect for You? 197

Summary..198

CHAPTER 17: CLOSING OUT A CASE
WHEN THE JUDGMENT HAS BEEN MET...............199

You Won, but There Is Still Paperwork.....................................199

Summary..204

APPENDIX: AGLOSSARY OF LEGAL TERMS.........205

APPENDIX: BRESOURCES BY STATE 223

INFORMATION COMPILED JULY 2009 223

ALABAMA 223

ALASKA 224

ARIZONA...225

ARKANSAS...226

CALIFORNIA...226

COLORADO...228

CONNECTICUT 229

DELAWARE..229

DISTRICT OF COLUMBIA..230

FLORIDA 231

GEORGIA...232

HAWAII 233

IDAHO 234

ILLINOIS...234

INDIANA 235

IOWA 236

KANSAS...237

KENTUCKY 238

LOUISIANA 239

MAINE...240

MARYLAND...240

MASSACHUSETTS...241

MICHIGAN...242

MINNESOTA 243

MISSISSIPPI 244

MISSOURI...245

MONTANA 245

NEBRASKA 246

NEVADA...247

NEW HAMPSHIRE 248

NEW JERSEY 249

NEW MEXICO 249

NEW YORK... 250

NORTH CAROLINA... 251

NORTH DAKOTA... 252

OHIO... 253

OKLAHOMA 254

OREGON 255

PENNSYLVANIA.. 256

RHODE ISLAND.. 256

SOUTH CAROLINA 257

SOUTH DAKOTA 258

TENNESSEE 259

TEXAS... 260

UTAH 261

VERMONT 262

VIRGINIA.. 262

WASHINGTON 263

WEST VIRGINIA.. 264

WISCONSIN... 265

WYOMING 266

US TAX COURT 267

Nationwide Public Records 267

APPENDIX C 269

USER GROUPS, NEWSGROUPS
AND CHAT GROUPS 269

Google Groups...269

Yahoo Groups 269

Usenet..270

BIBLIOGRAPHY 271

AUTHOR BIOGRAPHY 281

INDEX 283

PREFACE

Most of us go through life having some disagreements. The latest argument may have been with a local merchant who promised free service when you bought its recommended brand, or perhaps it was with an auto manufacturer concerning an extra device you ordered from the factory. You may even have had a disagreement with your local Internal Revenue Service (IRS) agent over the taxes you owed for a small lottery winning three years ago.

When we interact with other people or businesses in this country, we have a remedy for disputes called the small claims court. It is often a fast, hassle-free way to resolve life's little problems without the need to file a major lawsuit or hire an attorney. Explaining how to do this was the objective for writing this book.

This book, unlike the vast majority on the market, is designed for readers everywhere in the United States. It also has references and information on the only federal small claims court — the Small Claims Tax Court. The book illustrates how to win your case and effectively collect your money after the judge issues the paperwork that says you are right. Also included are examples of cases from people like you and information about how to find assistance when you desperately need it.

As business is transacted, as individuals agree to act together, and as limited liability companies and corporations supply services, conflicts will be created. It is a natural part of living in a free market system. Some disputes will be large and others small. Minor disputes can be settled in small claims court. What is "small" varies from state to state, so check the resources sections in Appendix B for the limits and costs of filing in your state.

Figure 1.1: Small Claims Court Checklist should help you learn the process, digest the terms, and move swiftly to get your case going. You will need to take a few steps to take your case to court and get back the money you have lost. This book will even detail various ways in which the defendant has the right to defend himself or herself from a court judgment that goes against him or her. As with all legal actions, there are often appeals or other trials you can propose to settle the matter to your satisfaction.

FIGURE 1.1: SMALL CLAIMS COURT CHECKLIST		
	To Do	√
1	Review state-by-state resources in this book.	
2	Do you have a case?	
3	Is the defendant judgment-proof?	
4	Write a formal demand letter to defendant.	
5	Try to settle out of court.	
6	Consider arbitration or mediation.	
7	Obtain forms from the Internet or court clerk.	
8	Establish venue and verify with court clerk.	
9	Get any free legal assistance available.	
10	Consider low cost local bar assistance.	
11	Prepare court documents.	
12	Arrange for service on the defendant.	
13	Organize your case.	
14	Obtain court assistance in getting evidence and witnesses.	√
15	Obtain direct testimony witnesses.	
16	Consider the need for "expert witnesses."	
17	Prepare for defendant's pretrial actions.	
18	Collect evidence with a clear chain of custody.	
19	Prepare a case notebook.	
20	Outline and write an opening statement.	
21	Outline and write evidence and document presentation.	

FIGURE 1.1: SMALL CLAIMS COURT CHECKLIST		
22	Outline and write your witnesses' examination.	
23	Outline and prepare notes on possible defense actions.	
24	Prepare to cross-examine with issues from a facts list.	
25	Outline and write a closing statement.	
26	Go to court and listen to other cases.	
27	Rehearse your case.	
28	Prepare a strategy if you lose.	
29	Prepare a strategy to collect the judgment.	
30	Get court assistance in finding assets and collecting your judgment.	

CHAPTER 1:

A WORLD FULL OF DISPUTES

WHO CAN YOU SUE?

In most cases, if you or your company has a dispute, you can settle it in small claims court — if the person or entity can be sued. This includes all individuals, whether individually, as a married couple, or named separately in a group. You may sue a business, even if it is organized as a corporation, limited liability company (LLC), a sole proprietorship, or a "Doing Business As" (DBA) company. Nonprofit organizations can also be sued.

In some states "class action" cases take place, where you sue to represent a group of similarly affected but unnamed plaintiffs. However, often, the big cost in this type of case is that of locating and paying all the plaintiffs. For this, the court may order an attorney or collection firm to do the distribution of the class action settlement.

If you have a tax problem with the IRS, it has a special small claims court in the larger cities of most states. The limit is $50,000 and applies to each tax year. In most cases, the IRS audits occur near the three-year statute of limitations on honest tax mistakes. The statute of limitations on tax fraud is five years or longer. In Small Claims Tax Court, you can file suits totaling $150,000 if the IRS is seeking back tax underpayments for the last three years available under the statute of limitations. You can sue the estate of a deceased individual by suing the executor of the estate within the time deadlines of estate law.

You cannot sue most government agencies unless they give prior approval to the suit. This kind of permission is rare. You also cannot sue members of the military or their families, whether they are overseas or in the United States. Prisoners in most states and also federal prisoners are exempt from suit in small claims court. To sue a minor, you must sue his or her parent(s). In most states, people who are disabled, either through physical or mental defect, cannot be sued.

WHAT KINDS OF LAWSUITS ARE POSSIBLE?

The common types of small claims court cases include negligence with automobiles, contract disputes, landlord or tenant issues, bad check issues, dog bite cases, property damage issues, personal injury cases, defective products cases, breach of warranty issues, and nuisance claims. Less common types of cases you can take to a court without a lawyer (pro se, acting as your own attorney) include divorce, child support, custody of a minor, professional malpractice, libel, slander, and defamation of character.

Most of these cases can be taken to small claims court if the amount of money involved meets the state's guidelines. Cases that deal with divorce and family matters are often conducted in family court. Pro se cases are fairly common. There are two additional exceptions to matters that can be brought before a local small claims court. First, cases dealing with an IRS decision, which requires you to pay money for taxes you do not feel you owe, may be taken to Small Claims Tax Court (see information for your state in Appendix B). Here, you may also be able to obtain a mediator for free, who will work with you and the IRS agent in charge of your case to resolve or compromise a solution before your day in court.

Second, if you obtain a judgment in a state court and are still unable to collect what is due to you under the various state law tactics described in the following sections, try going to Small Claims Tax Court. You will need to obtain the debtor's Social Security or federal identification number; then sue to attach the next available tax refund or overpayment.

THE RULE OF LAW

The rule of law dates back to the Magna Carta in the British Empire and is carried forth in American law and justice to this day. The rule of law says that no man is above the law. In the case of the small claims court, anyone can be sued, and he or she must appear before the judge, who hears both sides of a case. The rule of law is the leveling principle of our jurisprudence. All issues of dispute between two parties can be brought before a court with the proper venue. The cases in this book go before the small claims portion of the court system.

THE PSYCHOLOGY OF LITIGATION

In each small claims case, the parties have roles. The plaintiff is the aggressor who asserts his or her claim against the defendant, who tries to defend his or her position against the accusations of the plaintiff. It is plaintiff's responsibility to take every step necessary to push the case forward to a favorable decision. This includes a well-organized case, good evidence, controlled chain of custody of the evidence, the availability and use of witnesses, and an aggressive effort to counter the tactics of the defendant to disprove the case.

The defendant's role is more difficult psychologically when a person is accused of an act he or she does not want acquaintances to know about. This can be devastating. The actions a defendant must initiate in court are somewhat simpler than those of the plaintiff. The defendant must anticipate the alleged facts and evidence the plaintiff will present and then proceed in preparing statements, a testimony, or witnesses to disprove the allegation.

Whether you are the defendant or the plaintiff, a key to winning is to be polite when presenting statements, interrogating witnesses, or discussing evidence. Do not be rude, obnoxious, or loud. If you can force your opponent to make the case into a crusade, that may be enough to win points with some judges.

When filing a case, the psychological effect is to make the case a challenge to both sides. First, consider taking other steps that are available for settlement. When a plaintiff becomes disconcerted with normal means to reconcile a dispute, he or she will become resolute to the cause of using small claims court to settle matters. When a defendant is served with court documents, it is like a legal slap across the face, inviting the person to a joust. Both parties must keep their feelings hidden so that they may carry forth their cases in a calm, orderly fashion.

THE JUDGMENT-PROOF DEFENDANT

A judgment-proof defendant is a defendant who, regardless of the outcome of a lawsuit, will not have the means or inclination to pay the judgment that is ordered. Eighty-seven percent of the small claims court cases in the United States are never completely collected. In Appendix B: Resources by State, you will find links to national asset location services. You can save money in the long run by having a service check to see if the proposed defendant has the assets and income to pay the amount you expect to receive from small claims court.

Some defendants are automatically classed as "judgment-proof defendants." They include persons living on government-funded fixed incomes; persons with negative net worth; prisoners; members of the military service; and some state, federal, and local government agencies. Various groups may not be judgment-proof if they have insurance covering the type of action in which you are accusing involvement or entities with a guarantor (see Appendix A: Glossary of Legal Terms).

THE NEED FOR THIS BOOK

This book was designed to help those who want to redress a grievance by using a small claims court in their state. Check the limits for small claims cases in Appendix B in the back of the book. If your case is larger than the upper limit, you should hire an attorney and file a regular civil suit.

Reconsider going to court alone if you do not have the time to manage the process of preparing a complaint for the court, having your opponent served with the necessary papers, spending time watching other trials, practicing the presentation of your case, or dedicating at least a half-day to the trial itself. You are starting what could be a complicated procedure in collecting the debt created by a winning judgment.

The first choice in handling the case might be to hire an attorney. It will save what may be valuable time for you and increase your odds of securing money at the end. In some cases, the attorney's fees may be paid out of the settlement. If you feel you have the time necessary but want someone to take care of the paperwork, check in your state's section of Appendix B for companies that will file the paperwork for you. Show up in adequate time, and dress neatly on the court date. Act confident, and be prepared to present your case before the judge.

Because the major issue in most cases is the collection of the debt created by the judgment, you may wish to do all upfront work yourself and let a collection agency secure the debt. Most reputable collection agencies do not charge a fee but get a percentage of what they collect. Therefore, their services cannot put you further in the hole. Although this will reduce your compensation, you may consider your time to be worth the collection costs.

Many local bar associations and young lawyer groups will refer you to a low cost or free attorney, who will offer advice about the soundness of your case before you spend any money or time on it. A half-hour consultation with a junior member of a large law firm or a new practice started by a lawyer recently out of law school can cost as little as $35. The local attorney association in your area will find a low cost or free attorney for you if you call its office. This is an inexpensive way to be assured that you have a sound case that can end with the judgment and recovery of loss you hope to obtain.

CHAPTER 2:

PREPARING FOR SMALL CLAIMS COURT

The first step in any dispute between two parties is the writing or exchanging of demand letters. This action defines the basic facts of the dispute for both parties to read. It suggests that if a settlement is not forthcoming, a lawsuit will be prepared. Several sample demand letters and responses are provided in this book. The formula for a demand letter, which is a prerequisite to filing a lawsuit, will vary depending on the type of case.

When you go to small claims court, the judge will verify you have made your case for retribution to the other side before you brought the case to court. The court values its time and does not want to be the first forum for a dispute. To satisfy this, you could contact the other party in the dispute by phone or in person to notify them of your action. But, unless these notices to the potential defendant were witnessed, they cannot be submitted as evidence in court. A demand letter serves as direct evidence of a dispute.

FIGURE 2.1: SAMPLE AUTO ACCIDENT DEMAND LETTER
James Parkwood
7 Chutney Lane
Laguna Beach, CA XXXXX
August 27, 20XX
Ms. Katherine Russell
45 Cattlehorn Drive
Irvine Ranch, CA XXXXX

FIGURE 2.1: SAMPLE AUTO ACCIDENT DEMAND LETTER

Dear Ms. Russell,

As you may recall, on June 13 of this year, I was stopped at the intersection of High Drive and Pacific Coast Highway. As my car was stopped on High Drive, the signal light changed, which allowed me to turn right onto Pacific Coast Highway. You were traveling at a high speed and failed to stop at the red light that you were facing. You struck the rear passenger side of my car and hit a parked car owned by Ms. Melissa Carlson as she watched safely from the curb.

After I called the city police from my cell phone, you were issued a citation for driving while intoxicated (DWI), failure to stop at the red light, and reckless driving. I found out that you presented an expired insurance card for insurance coverage. The insurance company has indicated that you are an uninsured motorist after its search of the public insurance files.

Because I need my car for work, I have been forced to pursue repair work as soon as possible. I have gotten four bids and started work with the lowest body shop, which is for $1,298.24. I have included all bids and the police citation you received. I also have a copy of the required accident report, which we filed along with my potential co-plaintiff Ms. Carlson.

I would appreciate receiving a check as soon as possible. If you need to discuss any aspect of this accident, please give me a call at 555-8911, evenings.

Sincerely,

James Parkwood

FIGURE 2.2: SAMPLE AUTOMOBILE REPAIR DISPUTE DEMAND LETTER

Magic Auto Repair
771 Old Highway 42 West
Seadtick, KY XXXXX
June 15, 20XX

Dear Mr. Magic,

On June 2, 20XX, I brought my car to you for a regular oil change and lubrication. At that time, the mechanic, Jim Thorn, suggested that the mileage indicated I also

FIGURE 2.2: SAMPLE AUTOMOBILE REPAIR DISPUTE DEMAND LETTER

needed to have the tires rotated. He estimated the total job, including my favorite Bestex Synthetic Oil, to cost $55 plus tax on parts only. I signed the estimate and waited in the waiting room reading *Hunters Weekly*.

About 45 minutes later, Mr. Thorn reappeared with a problem. He said that during the inspection and tire rotation, he discovered a damaged wheel rim. Because he implied that the rim was a potential safety hazard, I asked what the new estimate would be if the rim were replaced with a new, original equipment, manufacturer's rim. The new estimate was $190 plus tax on parts only, and I signed the amended estimate to approve the work.

The work took another 45 minutes, and on my way out, I paid the cashier. I picked up the keys and drove the car about eight miles to my home in Fork Creek. As I negotiated the major turns on the road, I felt a vibration coming from the left front tire where the rim had been replaced. Because your shop was closed by the time I got home, I waited until the next day to return the car to you to troubleshoot the problem.

After I waited about an hour, again reading the same *Hunters Weekly*, Mr. Thorn returned to say he could find no physical indication there was a problem. He said he had road-tested the car in town for about ten minutes and not found the car created any vibration from the left front tire or rim.

While driving the car on the way home, I felt the vibration again. If you will recall, Mr. Magic, I called you and asked for your help in resolving the problem.

You told me that Mr. Thorn was a certified mechanic and that you considered the problem resolved. When I protested, you indicated that I was welcome to try another authorized dealer for repairs in the future.

I immediately did what you recommended and arranged for a repair at the dealership in Cary. They told me that the rim, which you replaced, was not a new original manufacturer's part, and, furthermore, it was the wrong size. They charged me $157.73 to install the tire on the proper rim, then rebalance and align the wheels.

When I returned to your dealership with my receipts and the incorrectly sized rim that plainly had a generic rim manufacturer's brand on it, you refused to refund any or the entire overcharge. You said the rim was never installed there and could not be returned to them.

FIGURE 2.2: SAMPLE AUTOMOBILE REPAIR DISPUTE DEMAND LETTER

I am now demanding that you repay me for the replacement costs for a defective and inferior-branded rim for my car. If you do not pay the $157.73 that I paid to the Cary dealer, which was a direct result of Mr. Thorn's, your employee, error, I shall take the matter to court. If this, indeed, becomes necessary, I shall seek any compensatory and/or punitive damages that are allowed in our state. It would be far cheaper and less trouble to issue me a check before July 30, 20XX.

Sincerely yours,

Justin Goodfellow

FIGURE 2.3: SAMPLE BREACH OF CONTRACT DEMAND LETTER

Melvin Peterson
13561 Golf Course Green
Louisville, KS XXXXX

May 22, 20XX

Mercer Martin
1441 Main Street
St. Louis, KS XXXXX

Dear Mr. Martin,

This letter is a follow-up to our recent phone conversation about the Elite Series electric golf cart I purchased from you on January 22, 20XX, following the ad you ran in the local newspaper (photocopy attached). The ad read "hardly used — almost new, perfect service record, excellent condition."

In review, I called and talked to you and asked why the unit was priced at only $1,500. You told me you needed immediate cash for your sister's medical bills. The next day, when I tried out the unit, you told me it had every recommended service, had recently been re-tired with the highest grade of golf-course tread tires, and had been used for only a few hours.

Relying on your statements, I bought the unit and rented a trailer to haul it to my home, which is off the ninth green of Karly Heights Golf and Country Club. As soon as I got the golf cart to my mechanic, he told me the brakes were about to fail and the transmission was in need of an overhaul. The mechanic indicated the cart had at least 10,000 hours on it and had likely been used in a rough and dusty environment, such as a landfill or junkyard.

FIGURE 2.3: SAMPLE BREACH OF CONTRACT DEMAND LETTER

I have had several mechanics look at the vehicle, and the lowest estimate I can find to put it back into safe running condition is $2,175. When I called you recently asking for a refund and return of the golf cart, you said, "All sales are final with me. It is always buyer beware these days."

This is my final demand for return and refund privileges on the golf cart. Failing that, I will have it repaired and go to small claims court (at 880 College Street) for the $2,175 in repair costs.

Sincerely,

Melvin Peterson

FIGURE 2.4: SAMPLE BREACH OF CONTRACT RESPONSE

Mercer Martin

1441 Main Street

St. Louis, KS XXXXX

May 28, 20XX

Melvin Peterson

13561 Golf Course Green

Louisville, KS XXXXX

Dear Mr. Peterson,

We both know your letter of May 22nd was the result of a vivid imagination and designed to take this matter where you think it belongs — the small claims court. As you know from the warranty information I furnished you with when you purchased the now disputed golf cart, the cart was originally purchased from the Johnson Golf Cart Service Company in Louisville.

I have spoken to Mr. Johnson. He said that he has complete service records on the golf cart you purchased from me. He confirmed that any brake or transmission work needed would fall under the warranty. As I told you on the phone, there is no need to either refund your money or spend the $2,175 to have it repaired. Those costs, if truly needed, will be covered at no cost to you. Just take the cart to Johnson Golf Cart Service Company..

FIGURE 2.4: SAMPLE BREACH OF CONTRACT RESPONSE

As to the veiled threats that you made on the phone about suing me for the funds in question, Mr. Johnson has kindly offered to be a witness for me to substantiate my claim that the cart was positively one that had little use. He can furnish repair documentation from my visits to Johnson Golf Cart Service from the time of original purchase to the time it was sold to you.

Please understand — I do not wish to be the pushy individual you portray me to be. However, if you decide to take this matter to court, I will countersue for my costs in defending this matter. I will seek recovery of any wages I lose as a result of your not following the only rational course in this case. In addition, if I have to miss my last few visits to my dying sister, I will sue for punitive damages.

Sincerely,

Mercer Martin

Enclosed: Copy of warranty from dealer, copies of letter from J. Hal Johnson in reference to golf cart serial number HI109-U892-2265.

FIGURE 2.5: SAMPLE BAD CHECK DEMAND LETTER

Carleston-Blaine Construction, Inc.

4571 Jerrison Pike

Dayton, MT XXXXX

January 21, 20XX

Jim Hemming Enterprises, LLC.

P.O. Box 4233

Clive, SD XXXXX

RE: Payment of Your $1,500 NSF Check # 1422

Dear Mr. Hemming,

Your company and mine were subcontractor and general contractor on a construction job related to the kitchen upgrades to the Holston Family Diner here in Dayton. When my subcontract was completed, I was paid by check number 1422.

FIGURE 2.5: SAMPLE BAD CHECK DEMAND LETTER

This check was returned non-sufficient funds (NSF) three times. This meets the limit that my bank will process an NSF item. I have been charged a total of $75 in bank charges, plus labor costs to type and mail this letter of $15.

Please remit immediately in certified funds the amount of $1,590 to cover these costs and the amount of the check, which are now due under the state's bad check laws. If you fail to remit within 30 days of this letter, I shall file a lawsuit in our small claims court and put *lis pendens* against the construction site so that you will not be able to get your final payment. I shall await your response, as this is about to destroy a longtime working relationship between our two companies.

Sincerely yours,

Mike Simon

President

Before you start any legal action, you should formally notify the other side that you plan to pursue the matter in court if necessary. This process is normally handled through the issuance of demand and response letters (see **Figure 2.1: Sample Auto Accident Demand Letter**, **Figure 2.2: Sample Automobile Repair Dispute Demand Letter**, **Figure 2.3: Sample Breach of Contract Demand Letter**, **Figure 2.4: Sample Breach of Contract Response**, and **Figure 2.5: Sample Bad Check Demand Letter**). Even if you have spoken with your opponent on the phone or in person, a demand letter and a response letter becomes part of the documentation for the case.

The letter should start by recalling any information that has happened in the past and that is not documented on paper. If you have paper documentation, acknowledge and attach copies. This puts the other party on notice that you will bring these into court as evidence. If you have witnesses, mention their names. Be precise on dates, times, and witnesses. If there is a written, verbal, or implied contract, indicate it in the letter.

In **Figure 2.1: Sample Auto Accident Demand Letter**, note the potential co-plaintiff knows that the other party was determined to be at fault by the police. This presents a possibly powerful witness, along with written documentation of the legal citation issued by the officer. The reference to the potential defendant's expired auto insurance indicates that another crime or legal liability may exist. Some states have uninsured motorist laws that suspend driving privileges to those in an accident without insurance. In this letter, the potential plaintiff asks the other party to call him to avoid the necessity of going to court. The letter says plainly that the plaintiff needs his automobile for commuting to work and, thus, could claim the consequential damage of loss of wages if the other party does not respond.

In the demand letter in **Figure 2.2: Sample Automobile Repair Dispute Demand Letter**, the potential plaintiff ends by threatening both compensatory and punitive damages. Although these damages are rare in small claims court, they are available in some states. In the demand letter, the threat adds to the seriousness of the ultimatum put forth by the damaged party's case. In this potential case, the influence of an authorized dealer as a possible witness adds to the validity that the part sold was not an authorized replacement part. The fact that the potential plaintiff is willing to compromise for only his out-of-pocket costs tells the judge he is a reasonable claimant. He appears to be making a conscious effort to avoid the time and expense of going to small claims court. The letter suggests that the plaintiff has the faulty tire rim and can prove it was the wrong brand.

We have the outline of a breach of an implied contract case in the next two letters. The initial demand letter, shown in **Figure 2.3: Sample Breach of Contract Demand Letter**, appears to mean serious business, because the plaintiff's demand letter even gives the street address where the case will be tried. The complaining party presented the newspaper ad that enticed him into buying the golf cart. Later, when he had the item reviewed by his mechanic, they found brake and transmission problems.

In **Figure 2.4: Sample Breach of Contract Response**, the potential defendant responds by saying the facts presented in the ad can be substantiated and that if there are any brake or transmission repairs needed, they are still covered under the original manufacturer's warranty. The defendant is adamant that he did not misrepresent the item sold and, more important, offers a remedy that will cost the potential plaintiff nothing to resolve any defects in the golf cart.

The last demand letter, shown in **Figure 2.5: Sample Bad Check Demand Letter**, indicates a collection problem and a breach of contract case. The potential plaintiff is an unpaid subcontractor for a construction job and, therefore, can file a mechanic's lien or *lis pendens* against the real property on which he worked. This is an indirect course to obtain his money. The building owner may have paid the contractor for the subcontractor's work, but the contractor supplied the subcontractor a check with insufficient funds in the bank to back it up. The potential plaintiff attempts to end the letter on a conciliatory note by suggesting it is better business for both parties for this to be settled outside of court. The subcontractor may be so well known that his presence at a bid can win the job for the general contractor.

DOES YOUR LOSS FIT THE LIMITS OF SMALL CLAIMS COURT?

The monetary limits are listed as the first item under your state in Appendix B. If you live in an area near another state and are doing business across state lines, check both states for jurisdiction and monetary limits. Normally, the rules deal either with the location in which the transaction occurred or the address of the potential defendant's residence or place of business. In some cases, you will find there is a possibility that you can sue for the full loss in one state, while you may be limited by the monetary limits in another state. In any case, the monetary limits are what the state allows, and you cannot split your case into two suits to collect more money. However, if you have a choice of jurisdictions and one has a higher limit, check to see if you can file your suit there.

If a payment was made by a credit card and it has been made within nine months, you should file a dispute with the credit card company. You may start the dispute and have the money withdrawn from the disputed person's credit card account with a simple phone call. You may still owe the money, even though it is held in abeyance until the matter is settled with a decision by the credit card company. A form will be sent for you to fill out and outline your dispute. Be sure to provide copies of any requested documents, as well as other information that would facilitate a settlement of the issues in the dispute.

Early in any potential small claims court case, the complainant needs to evaluate the legal merit of his or her claim. Web sites such as **www.lawyers.com** and **www.learnaboutlaw.com** provide useful forums where you can ask questions and receive answers from practicing attorneys. A site that California Small Claims Judges, Pro Tem, use to guide their decisions is found at **www2.courtinfo.ca.gov/protem,** and it is useful for most small claims cases anywhere. These sites, along with your local bar association, will find local lawyers who can give you a free or low cost evaluation of your case. In some jurisdictions, the court provides a legal adviser to assist you in analyzing your claim and suggests ways to improve your chances of winning in court. If you do not feel strongly enough about the issues of the dispute to seek advice on the case's merit and standing before the court, think twice about filing the case.

Often a visit to your state's small claims Web site or local court clerk's office will get you the forms you need to file and also an explanation of what costs can and cannot be claimed in your state's court. Well-documented direct costs are always covered up to the monetary limit of the small claims court in your state. Some indirect costs may also be allowed if the total — after these claims are added — is still under the state's mandated upper limit of small claims cases. You may be compensated for loss of work; pain and suffering; and also medical costs, repair, and court costs. Be apprised that you may have to reimburse any medical cost compensation to the health insurance carrier that paid the bills while you were injured or in the hospital.

SHOPPING FOR THE BEST FORUM

If, when adding up the costs you expect to be part of a judgment, you discover that those exceed the monetary limits of your state's small claims court, consider hiring an attorney and letting him or her file a lawsuit on your behalf in the regular civil court. Although you can act pro se in this court as well, you will find the court and its rules are tighter and more difficult. If a case is considerably large, it is highly recommended that you seek assistance from a professional. In some cases, state civil courts will award legal fees as part of the judgment.

In cases where there are intangible costs, such as pain and suffering, the court can often use its wide discretion in deciding what is due in the judgment. This threat of a large judgment may cause the opposition to compromise and pay part of the total amount you sought originally. In these cases, attorneys often negotiate payment of the winning party's attorney fees and costs in addition to what you receive. In such cases, your opponent will have to pay your attorney's court-approved and reasonable costs.

GETTING STATE FORMS AND FILING WITH THE COURT

When asked, your local court clerk's office will often direct you to a Web site where the necessary forms for small claims court can be downloaded or prepared online. The forms are often found in portable document format (PDF) that you can download and edit on your computer. Most state sites have PDF file readers available for free so you can read the PDF forms. Alternately, when downloaded, the forms can be printed so that you may fill them out by hand. However, this is not recommended. Make your claim look more professional by editing it with a word processor. Most word processors, such as WordPerfect and Word, have built-in functions to fill in PDF forms.

If you do not have a word processor capable of reading and editing a PDF file, you can obtain one for free from many "open system" freeware sites. An open system, Word-compatible software download site is www.download. openoffice.org/index.html. A professional-looking claim filed with the court will start your case in a positive direction. Research and prepare all essential documents for the case before submitting your petition to the court.

If your case requires the presence of witnesses who may not appear unless ordered to do so by the court, prepare necessary subpoenas. If you need documents or evidence that you have not accumulated, subpoena them from whomever has the items. Documents you can readily obtain yourself, such as police reports, should be available if you need to attach them to the petition. If mediation is required, prepare any documents or witness subpoenas you may need for this pretrial phase.

The court clerk will arrange service on the other party(s) to the action and all witnesses. You may have a choice as to the means of service. Often, service by mail fails because the potential defendant simply refuses the registered letter. Service by the county sheriff or marshal may not work because the service of papers may be a low priority in an office that is busy with criminal matters. Even though commercial service agents are more costly, they tend to be diligent in their efforts to complete service to the correct person.

Before preparing your forms and going to the court clerk's office, consider looking at some of the commercial Web sites that do the case preparation and filing for you. They may offer you a package that is quite economical, considering all the items it includes. A simple Web search for "small claims court" will locate these sites in the advertised links at the top or sides of the search findings.

If you have a choice of court dates, select the date that is most convenient for you. Some small claims courts meet weekly, while others offer day and night sessions to accommodate most workers' schedules. Remember to allow enough time for the defendant to be served. The law may require a waiting period after this service for the defendant to file a countersuit or answer the complaint. Prepare as well as possible before the court date, and hope that the defendant will be unable to bring a strong case on the scheduled trial date.

Some states allow a jury trial in a small claims court case. You should decide if this is more advantageous. Jury trial cases take more time than those decided by a judge. Cases where the defendant claims justification for his or her actions are often more successful with juries. Cases that rise and fall strictly on the basis of the facts, presented in an unambiguous manner, are better brought before a judge. If you have a choice, weigh the circumstances carefully before you ask for a jury trial.

SUMMARY

This chapter should have given you some insight into the drafting of a demand letter. Even if it is not required in your state, it is a good idea to have this letter in a small claims case. First, the letter offers the potential defendant a chance to settle, with both of you compromising instead of going to trial. Second, it provides good evidence in court to prove to the judge that you tried to resolve the issue before going to court. Using the material in this chapter, you should have been able to locate the specific limits and rules of your state, the costs of a small claims lawsuit, and the local source for filing and hearing the case.

You should now be aware that there are other ways to solve disputes and that the court may impose legal means, such as mediation, on the dispute before you are allowed to go to court. You should comprehend the limits of your small claims court and the proper venue for the dispute in question. Most state forms are available on the Internet and can be downloaded to your computer. It is easy to use software you already own or to download the necessary software for free. It is important to furnish neat and correctly written filing papers. With the help of the court, you can find free or inexpensive legal assistance in preparing your case.

The small claims court process will allow countersuits or counterclaims. Each person will be allowed to present his or her side, and then a judgment will be made. Most states allow for either a retrial in small claims court or an appeal of the case to a higher court. This review may include a representation of the complete case in chief or just a review of the underlying law that formed the basis of the decision. Small claims courts never set new case law. If you win the case, you will still have to go through the process of collecting the debt created by the judgment. After receiving payment, notify the court that the matter has been settled as per the judgment ordered.

CHAPTER 3:

Do You Have a Good Case?

Before filing a lawsuit, you should do extensive legal research to feel positive about having your case tried in court. You need to be indubitably sure of the facts in the case. As you will recall from the demand letters in the previous chapter, the plaintiff and the defendant remember the facts differently. There are situations where there is so much doubt that a decision in court may not be possible.

For example, if a defendant feels the plaintiff has given him or her a menacing look, this might constitute a threat to inflict bodily harm. The frightened person may want to seek a restraining order and damages. In cases such as these, it is better to have verbal threats with witnesses present to have a good chance to win the case.

If your case has tangible evidence of injury, such as broken bones or other painful injuries, you likely will find you have a good case. Your injury case will be improved if there is physical damage in addition to bodily damage. For example, if there was damage to your automobile that occurred at the same time as your personal injury, you have a stronger case. Each added element of damage adds proof to the case you are trying to build.

However, even cases with physical damages and personal injury can be difficult to prove at trial. If you have an injury that the doctors diagnose as a "soft injury," it may be hard to win a case in court without an expert witness. Often, nonspecific injuries to the muscles, tendons, or other areas of the body make it difficult to document the degree of the injury. The case is improved by x-ray, magnetic resonance imaging (MRI), or computed axial tomography (CAT) scan information, with appropriate written commentary from your doctor or an expert witness.

When considering whether you have a good case, evaluate:

- **Evidence**: In court, it does not matter what truly happened. It is only significant what you can prove happened. Witnesses are critical. When witnesses from both sides agree on critical issues, your case is sound. If the critical issues are points of disagreement, your case may not be strong; therefore, you should consider any compromises that are on the table.

- **Legal proof**: If you go to court with a particular type of issue, you must know the key points the law requires you to prove before you can win a favorable verdict. For example, in an injury-by-automobile case if the defendant claims the cause was bad brakes, be sure you have sued both the driver and the company responsible for the brakes failing to work on the defendant's car. This way, if the judge rules in assigning fault, you will be the beneficiary of the judgment.

- **Adversary's story**: One of the advantageous aspects of a demand letter is that it elicits from your opponent his or her side of the story. As with our previous demand letters, response letters are rare, and you may face going to trial with no knowledge of the opponent's defense strategy.

- **"Damage control" defense**: When you sue for a wrongful act, such as malicious or wrongful termination of a job or employer discrimination, be prepared for a positive defense. As a defendant, the employer likely will plead that there were mitigating circumstances or perhaps misconduct for similar acts that initiated the cause for termination or penalty given to the offending employee. When possible, have other later cases of the wrongful act exposed by your witnesses. You should argue that after-the-fact changes are not a defense for wrongful conduct you received.

- **Malpractice coverage**: Some professionals, such as doctors, may carry insurance coverage against the malfeasance on which you are basing your suit. In advance, subpoena documentation of this coverage so that you can add the insurance company's name to your list of parties being sued. If your medical insurance covered all or part of your medical costs, subpoena the records to see what specialties the doctor is said to be capable of practicing. If you find the listed specialties do not match the doctor's credentials, add your carrier as a named defendant. The carrier is liable for his or her certification of ability.

- **Frivolous lawsuit**: The Federal Rules of Civil Procedure advise potential plaintiffs that they must have evidentiary support for the claims of their case. A case where the defendant claims he has been bitten many times by a neighbor's dog, without any pictures of the bites, scars, or records of treatment by a professional, might be classified as a "malicious prosecution." If you sue that defendant for the same cause at different points in time without winning a case, this may be considered an "abuse of process," and the case may result in damage being awarded to the defendant.

GETTING HELP IN ANALYZING YOUR CASE DETAILS

Getting help with your first case — or any case for that matter — is often a critical first step. Initially, try the court clerk's office for information of what legalities may have been broken by your particular case. Some offices have law students available to assist in answering basic questions. As suggested, go to Appendix B for Web sites that will give you a reference to a free or low cost attorney who will spend a worthwhile half-hour with you. In some states, the filing fees, service fees, and costs can total as much as $350 for a single small claims case. Although most states are more reasonable, the small fee you may have to pay a young attorney in analyzing your case is cheap insurance against having an unwinnable case on your trial day.

The questions at issue in the review of your case are as follows:

- **Which rule of law is at issue?** You should either read or have explained to you the law pertaining to the type of claim you will be presenting in court. You or your attorney can go to a local law library and review the sections of the law that deal with the dispute you have with the defendant.

- **State law**: In most cases, the dispute will fall under a state or local statute. This law will be used by the small claims court to accept or reject your arguments for a judgment against the defendant. If you have your case reviewed by an attorney, ask which specific section was violated and what case law supports your case. The state law is written by state legislative bodies and revised over time into a unified volume of law, which will have a different name in each state.

- **Case law**: Each section of the law will have cases established by higher courts to define what the statute truly means. If you can cite the section of law and specific cases that support your claim, you will increase your chance of winning your case.

- **Local law**: In some cases, the law supporting your case is a local ordinance. For example, laws that control pets are often local laws. If local laws establish something as illegal, this may give you the right to sue for negligence under that ordinance. Check with your local law advisory or animal control officer.

- **Federal law**: In most cases, you cannot use federal law directly in a local small claims court; however, many federal laws have state counterparts. For example, employee discrimination is a federal protection granted to workers based on age, sex, race, and sexual orientation. Most states have duplicate or similar laws that you can use as a basis for a small claims court case.

- **Does the statute of limitations apply?** The statute of limitations for your case depends on the type of dispute you have and the laws that regulate the conduct that has been breached by the dispute. If you are having your case reviewed by an attorney, ask the attorney. The law may have a statute of limitations that runs from the start of the act to the end of the act or to its last occurrence. Timing can be complicated. At a minimum, you should read the law and calculate the time that has passed since the occurrence took place. It is important to check the timing before you waste time or money on a case where time, under the statute of limitations, has run out. Be aware that the statute of limitations against a government agency may run out quicker than the rule for all other defendants under a given law.

- **What court has the power to hear the case?** Appendix B outlines where you may file a case in your state. In some states, you have more than one choice. In areas near state lines, you may be able to file the case in adjacent states if the defendant either resides or has a business located there. A case based on an event that occurred in another state may have to be filed there. When you have a choice of filing out-of-state, you should be aware of the possibility of being viewed as a "carpetbagger" in that jurisdiction.

- **What about mediation or arbitration?** Some cases, such as a breach of contract case, may have sections in the contract requiring disputes that arise out of the contract to be decided by either mediation or arbitration. In some states, a mediation process is required before the actual trial may occur. In certain cases, the use of mediation may be in the interest of both parties. It may allow a faster decision and keep the parties from holding long-term animosities.

WHOM TO SUE

Most disputes start between two persons. People may act as representatives to a business, nonprofit group, or government agency. The business may be a foreign corporation, a U.S. corporation outside your state's border, a corporation based in your state, a sole proprietorship, or a limited liability corporation. You must locate the exact legal entity or person you wish to serve. You should also serve any guarantors or insurance companies that may be involved in the liability.

If you paid the individual by check, look at the endorsement, and have your bank trace where it was deposited. If you received an invoice, use the company name on it. If you had a contract, use the name shown on the contract. If the job was done on the basis of a bid, the paperwork should show the legal name of the party, which you would list as the defendant. If the dispute arose out of an automobile accident or purchase, use the names on the title or registration of the car. If you have insurance, add any policy numbers on the proof of insurance. If the dispute is with a bonded vender, include the company holding the bond as a defendant.

STEPS TO THE COURT CLERK'S DOOR

In some states, you can file a small claims court application from your home by using a computer. You can select the form, fill in the boxes, and pay all court fees and service costs by credit card from a secure Web page. If you are in a state with a standard PDF form for all state courts, you may download it and fill in the information on your computer as previously outlined.

The court in some states will allow you to use a printed form with handwritten or typed information on it. If possible, neatly type the documentation. A few states accept small claims cases using only the forms that attorneys routinely use for their civil law cases. If you are in one of those states, you will need a local filing service or paralegal service firm to type the form. You should be able to find these services in your local phone book or with an Internet search for "(your city) paralegal."

FIGURE 3.1: SAMPLE PDF TYPE CLAIM FILING

CASE NAME: MARTIN J. V. MILLER M. CASE # 45-98922-09

STEPS

1. The Plaintiff: ☑the person, ☐business, or ☐public entity that is suing is:

Name: John Miller   **Phone:** (555)555-1212

Street: 114 Cardwell Street   **City:** Halpin   **State:** MD

Mailing Address: Street: SAME   **City:**   **State:**

2. The Defendant: ☑the person, ☐business, or ☐public entity being sued is:

Name: Maryanne Miller   **Phone:** (555)555-2121

Street: 51223 State Route 74 West   **City:** Malpin   **State:** MD

Mailing Address: Street: **City:**   **State:**

3. The Plaintiff claims the Defendant owes $1,332.45

You must ask the Defendant (in person, in writing, or by phone) to pay you before you sue. Have you done this? ☑Yes ☐No — If not, why_____ .

4. Why are you filing your claim at this courthouse?

☑Where the Defendant lives or does business. ☐Where the Plaintiff's property was damaged. ☐Where the Plaintiff was injured.	☐Where a contract (written or spoken) was made, signed, performed, or broken by the defendant or where the Defendant lived or did business when the defendant made the contract.

FIGURE 3.1: SAMPLE PDF TYPE CLAIM FILING

5. Did you and the defendant attend mandatory mediation in this case?

If yes, and if you have had mediation, attach a copy of the finding ☐ attached; if not explain why._____Defendant was a no-show._____

☒No ☐Yes: A claim was filed on _____: If the public entity denies your claim or does not answer within the time allowed by law, you can file this form. If yes, you must file a written claim with the entity first.

7. Signed:

I swear this application to be true under the state laws.

_____John Miller_____ *John Miller*_____

Plaintiff types or prints name here   *Plaintiff signs here*

Figure 3.1 is a sample that has been shortened to represent only the information the court would need in a debt collection case. The sample has a typical questionnaire to determine if the case fits the court's jurisdiction.

First, enter your name and address. If you are representing a company or corporation, enter the name and place of business, and select the appropriate boxes. In most cases, if you select a box on your computer and touch the space key, it turns the box into a "X" or a "√." You are giving your identity and type of legal entity. This may determine your standing before the court. Although this form does not call for it, you may need to enter the date of filing and the date of the dispute on the form.

Second, enter the same type of information for the defendant. Some forms allow you to append extra copies of the information for other defendants. Be sure you have located the defendant and have his or her correct address. Appendix B offers several search sites for locating addresses of individuals and businesses. Remember to add guarantors or insurance companies to forms where appropriate.

The third step on this form is to provide the amount of the debt in question. In some states, this area of the form may request information on the underlying cause of the debt, such as a bad check. The importance of the demand letters mentioned previously cannot be emphasized enough. This form asks if a demand was made before the court was requested to intervene. The implementation of a demand letter is imperative.

Step four is all about the issue of venue. The form asks questions that will give the judge a simple criterion for deciding if the court has the venue necessary to hear the case. The court's first issue is always venue. After this is established, the court can hear the case, and the defendant cannot challenge venue. In a debt collection case, in many states, a valid debt can be challenged only if the court does have venue.

Next, the form asks about the state's mandatory mediation service for small claims. Plaintiffs are normally required to show up for mediation if they want the judge to hear the case. At a minimum, the plaintiff will not be able to collect a debt if he or she does not appear at the mediation session the court schedules for the case. In most cases, the defendant will not be held in default for failure to appear or automatically lose the case. However, failing to appear may be an act of bad faith. The defendant's failure to appear is not considered a fault of the plaintiff.

As indicated previously, a small claims court claim against a public agency may be different. In some states, the agency must agree to be the defendant. In other states, there is a short statute of limitations. Also, a simple denial of the claim will move the case to a different court in some cases. In this sample form, the plaintiff has not indicated that a public agency is involved in the case.

FIGURE 3.2: SAMPLE TYPED CIVIL COURT COMPLAINT
Carson Myer Route 3, Box 733 Green Ferry Road Coster, TN XXXXX 555-515-5100

FIGURE 3.2: SAMPLE TYPED CIVIL COURT COMPLAINT

Plaintiff Pro Per

The Superior Court of Pioneer Town

County of Hasterton

State of Tennessee

Carson Myer

        Plaintiff

       v.   Case Number_____

Keenan Williams   COMPLAINT

    Defendant   JURY TRIAL DEMANDED

1. On approximately April 19, 20XX, at 3:30 p.m., EST, while Plaintiff Carson Myer was riding his bicycle in the painted, signed, and marked bike path along Highway 232, the Scenic Old West Highway in Hasterton County, Defendant Keenan Williams did negligently enter the bike path with his car and struck the Plaintiff.

2. As a result of the Defendant's negligent driving, the Plaintiff's right leg and right arm were broken, causing substantial pain and suffering, loss of income, and medical expense.

WHEREFORE, Plaintiff prays for judgment against the defendant of $15,000 plus costs and interest.

Carson Myer
_____

Carson Myer, Plaintiff in Pro Per Plaintiff demands trial by jury

The seventh, and last, step for this PDF-type claim form is to sign and file it with the court. In cases where you file the case online from your personal computer, there is a process called electronic signing. When this occurs, the court takes note of your Internet carrier, the time, date, and your personal Internet address for this session on the computer. This type of signature is quite secure but can be faked by the technologically savvy.

Figure 3.2: Sample Typed Civil Court Complaint shows a type of format that is used in some state small claim courts and most civil courts in the United States. This form just requires the full name and addresses of the plaintiff and defendants, plus a brief outline of the claim and relief sought. Here the defendant demands a jury trial. The defendant claims he was hit while riding his bicycle in a bike path by the defendant's automobile and suffered $15,000 (the small claims limit) in actual damages, medical costs, and loss of income, as well as pain and suffering compensation.

ESTIMATING YOUR LOSS PLUS COSTS

Your suit in small claims court is limited by the maximum shown for your state in the Appendix B. Most states, within the overall limit, will allow you to include any direct costs associated with the dispute. This may include such points as repair or replacement costs for a defective or damaged item. Also included in most state's costs are the court costs and fees required to send the matter before the judge or magistrate in the small claims court.

As shown in **Figure 3.3: Sample County Clerk's Office Fee Chart**, small claims court costs can be complicated and expensive. Some states charge as a matter of public policy a low, standard, one-fee-covers-all assessment. Most charge for services on an as-needed basis. The purpose of each of these fees is given in Appendix A. The most common fees you will have to pay when going to court are as follows:

- **The filing fee:** This is a basic fee for managing the claim within the court's office. It covers storing, scheduling the case, matching the case documents with other documents the court has processed, and bringing the file of necessary paperwork to the judge at the time of the trial.

- **Defendant service:** You will need to pay the court, the sheriff, or a private service to serve the defendant with the papers that order him or her to appear in court on the trial date.

- **Subpoena:** If you require evidence that is not in your hands or if you need to have hard-to-get witnesses — such as law enforcement officials or hostile witnesses — you will need a subpoena served on them to guarantee their presence at the trial.

- **Jury fee:** Although rare, some states charge plaintiffs part of the costs of gathering a jury to hear the case.

FIGURE 3.3: SAMPLE COUNTY CLERK'S OFFICE FEE CHART	
JUNE ASTER, COUNTY COURT CLERK	
COUNTY OF HAVERSON	
101 COURT HOUSE SQUARE	
MCMURREYVILLE, XX XXXXX	
Filing Fees	
Small claims court filing fee	$100
Transfer to district court	$250
Appeals	$100
Counterclaim	$ 50
Rent escrow	$ 75
Debt collection escrow	$ 65
Debtor examination	$ 75
Request for disclosure (per defendant)	$ 15
Request to show cause (per defendant)	$ 15
Miscellaneous Fees	
Certified copies	$ 10

FIGURE 3.3: SAMPLE COUNTY CLERK'S OFFICE FEE CHART	
Defendant service	$ 25
DWI chemical dependency assessment	$125
Exemption certificate (w/certified copy)	$ 40
Executions	$ 50
Fax filings (each 50 pages or part thereof)	$ 25
Judgment search (per name)	$ 5
Jury fee	$175
Motions and responses to motions	$ 50
Satisfaction of judgment	$ 5
Subpoena	$ 15
Transcript of judgment	$ 30
Summary of judgment	$ 20
Trust account filing	$ 45
Uncertified copies	$ 5
Writs	$ 40

As established by the Honorable County Council for the county of Haverson on the 1st day of June 20XX, to become effective on the 1st of July 20XX, or until revised by action of the County Council in a regular public meeting in the future.

- **Transcript or summary of judgment:** If you win the judgment, you will need either a transcript of judgment or a summary of judgment. These documents prove that the court has awarded you money.

- **A debtor examination:** If the defendant does not pay the judgment, one of the techniques of collection is to have the judge ask the defendant under oath where his assets are located.

- **Satisfaction of judgment**: After you have collected money from the defendant, you need to tell the court that its judgment has been satisfied by filing a paper for this purpose.

All these fees often can be collected from the defendant as a recovery of your cost to bring the suit. In some states, all or part of these fees can be waived for those who cannot pay them (See **Figure 3.4: Application for Waiver of Fees**). Occasionally, they must be repaid when the satisfaction of judgment is filed.

Some states allow indirect costs, such as loss of wages and compensation for pain and suffering, to be added if other direct costs are under the state's mandated limit. You should always add the direct costs and court fees before you estimate other eligible costs.

FIGURE 3.4: APPLICATION FOR WAIVER OF FEES

Application for Waiver of Fees

State of Nevada Standard Form

County of _____

Name of Applicant_____

Case Number_____

Approved by_____, Judge

I, the applicant above, after being properly placed under oath, do swear or affirm that I have no money or means to pay the filing fees and other associated costs with my lawsuit; that I believe my lawsuit asks the court for relief to which I am legally entitled; and that the following information is true and correct. I understand that if the information I provide below misleads the court in determining my insolvency, I may be subject to contempt of court or charged with the crime of perjury. Signed:_____

Employer: _____ Social Security # _____.

A. Monthly Income	B. Monthly Expenses
Wage income _____	Rent / Mortgage_____

FIGURE 3.4: APPLICATION FOR WAIVER OF FEES

Bonuses / Commissions_____	Insurance_____
Disability / Public Assistance _____	Utilities_____
Other Income_____	Repairs_____
A. Monthly Income total_____	Clothing_____
C. Assets	**B. Monthly Expenses**
Cash _____	Food_____
Stocks / Bonds _____	Auto Payments_____
Home _____	Other expenses_____
Auto _____	B. Total Monthly Expense_____
Other_____	D. Liabilities
C. Total Assets_____	Mortgage _____
	Auto Loan_____
	Other_____
FOR OFFICE USE BELOW THIS LINE	D. Total_____
A - B. Net Income Total_____	C – D. Net Worth Total_____
Approved by: _____	

When estimating such items as lost wages, be sure to get a witness or notarized statement from your employer who can give the court the exact figures. Anticipated overtime pay cannot be collected. If the company where you were working experienced a layoff due to an economic downturn, you will need to prove you would not have been affected if you were able to work.

A few states allow consequential, or punitive, damages to be added, within the state-mandated limit of a small claims case. If you are going to represent yourself in cases where these damages exist, you should study carefully the case law for your type of case. These damages may be calculated as a multiple of the direct costs, so you should obtain a sample case to cite to the judge that gives him guidance as to the reasonableness of your claim. Small claims courts do not establish case law or interpret state statutes on matters related to this type of claim.

MAKING YOUR CASE FIT STATE LIMITS

Although most state-mandated small claims limits leave little wiggle room for getting the full amount of your loss in bigger cases, there are other matters to consider. First, if the claim involves an auto accident covered by either your or the defendant's insurance, it is wise to hire an attorney who can file in a court without a monetary limit. Insurance companies may be unwilling to pay for soft injury costs, such as semi- or permanent pain associated with damage done to your body.

You should speak with an attorney who specializes in such cases. Your phone directory will display the specialty information. These attorneys often receive a percentage of the recovered settlement. Although there is no cost to you for their services if nothing is gained, these attorneys will put forth their maximum effort only if you pressure for a higher settlement. These attorneys work rapidly to win their cases to move on to new clients.

In cases where you have potential defendants with funds sufficient to cover your pain and suffering, you may wish to consider filing pro se in a higher court, where there is a higher maximum monetary amount. Be prepared to either negotiate an out-of-court settlement lower than you are seeking in court or find that the defendant hires an attorney to represent himself or herself in the higher court. In this case, you may have to either take the gamble of representing yourself or paying an attorney a retainer to represent you in court.

If your injury is job-related, contact your union representative if you have one. Unions will often pay for an attorney or have an attorney on their national office staff that can represent your case in a higher court, where small claims limits do not apply. If your case includes either workman's compensation or Social Security disability income issues, use an attorney who specializes in these matters. These attorneys often get a percentage of back income you lost because of your inability to work and the failure of program officials to grant timely benefits of workman's compensation or social security disability income. They work to retrieve money that you probably never would have obtained without their efforts.

Finally, if you are suing a firm with its headquarters in a nearby state with a higher state-mandated small claims court limit, you might consider filing there instead of your state. You cannot file both places, but sometimes, this allows you a choice of where to file a suit. You should consider the effect that moving the case will have on any positive or needed witnesses. If the witnesses have to pay to travel, plus lose a day's pay, they may not be as friendly. However, the defendant company may be more sensitive to lawsuits filed in its home state.

FREE RESOURCES FOR HELP

As indicated previously, you can find free resources at most small claims court clerk's offices and local bar association-sponsored community resources. Appendix B also lists sources of free information applicable to your state. There are many sources of help that you may find available to specific areas of the country. For example:

- **Large university libraries**: It is not uncommon for most state-supported universities to have a law program. Even those universities and colleges that do not may have a small law library. These are good resources for being able to research issues of where to file, the statute of limitations for your specific case, venue law, and issues involving case law. If the books you need are not in the public area of the library, you can often ask the reference librarian to get the necessary volumes from the back shelves. A librarian should oblige you by bringing the necessary books to a public reading room. Annotated copies of state law normally cannot be checked out of the library, so set aside extra time to study them there.

- **Law firm libraries**: Larger law firms in major cities have a necessary annotated reference set of the state laws in a central library or conference room. This makes it convenient for all members of the firm or law clerks to use when researching a client's case. It is not uncommon for these firms to make this reference room available on a limited basis to outside individuals doing pro se work. A phone call to the office receptionist will often put you in contact with an administrative assistant or paralegal, who can tell you the firm's policies on use of its law library. Similar to the rules of the university library, you will not be permitted to remove the books from the office. Be prepared to read and take notes to build your case at the firm's facility.

- **Online law libraries**: A simple Web search for "online law library" will return pages of links to Web site sources for the law you need to build your case. In many cases, you can find a law school or other sponsored library that has law resources available online. Do not avoid nearby out-of-state law schools, as many keep the legal information for all 50 states. Yahoo! has **www.dir.yahoo.com/ Government/law/legal_research/** libraries, but there are other dedicated resources.

- **Paralegal services**: Paralegal service firms can often provide low cost solutions to particular types of cases. A phone call to these listings in your local phone directory will tell you if these services can meet your need.

SUMMARY

This chapter directed you to study and locate the necessary evidence, laws, and previous cases that support your small claims case. You should have written a demand letter for your dispute and attempted to settle it through either an out-of-court settlement or mediation, if this is required in your state.

You should have obtained the necessary forms and legal assistance to be confident your case is sound. You should be sure you have the correct venue for the case. Research should have been done to assure you that the dispute is timely under the state's statute of limitations for the particular issue involved. Finally, you should have filed your case with the court and begun the process of service on the defendant and witnesses needed for trial. If you have been diligent in your efforts, you should be prepared for most issues that may arise before the actual trial.

CHAPTER 4:

Preparing for What Can Go Wrong

For most of us, the road to the small claims court can be bumpy and full of detours. Anticipating these irritations will make your solution more efficient and your life less stressful. If your dispute has gotten to the point of going to a court to settle the issues, both sides are likely locked into philosophies and views that their facts will not change. An understanding of what might happen between the time you file suit and the time you have your trial day is important.

DEFENDANT'S RIGHTS

The defendant has certain rights that can change what you would expect to be the next steps in your quest toward a favorable judgment in small claims court. These rights include:

Venue

The defendant(s) has the right to have his or her claims about the case heard in a court with the proper venue, but there are exceptions to the common rules of venue. For example, if a business defendant's presence in the jurisdiction where you filed the case is only by way of an independent dealer rather than a company-established place of business, the proper venue in some states would be where the company's main place of business resides. An individual defendant who has physically taken up residence in an out-of-state location may not be sued in his old place of residency. In most states, the issue is determined by the date and time of the dispute in question. If the venue is ruled to be incorrect, you will have to start over in the jurisdiction that has the proper venue.

Right to be Represented by Counsel

The defendant has an absolute right to acquire and use an attorney to represent his or her side of the case. The judge may allow the trial date to be reset so that the attorney selected can be brought up to date on the case. If the defendant elects to have an attorney represent him or her, it is a good idea to reconsider your status as a pro se plaintiff. If you decide to use an attorney, move swiftly, as the judge will not likely grant a second delay in the trial for you to obtain counsel.

Proper Service of the Defendant

The court will not hear a case until the defendant has been legally served. Absolute proof of service of the defendant by an independent person (someone not part of the case) is a minimum requirement. Normally, if a defendant appears in court and says that an unauthorized person accepted service, the court will require a new service of the defendant. However, if a defendant does not appear in court after a certified proof of service has been accomplished, a default judgment is normally issued in your favor. The defendant's later timely appearance before the court may void the default judgment and require the setting of a new future trial date. In some states, service must be perfected no fewer than a certain number of days before the trial date.

Alternate Solutions in Place of a Trial

Although you may not have been able to reach a solution to your dispute with the defendant before filing the small claims court papers, you may find alternatives to resolving the matter. There are some rights that a defendant must invoke to give him or her special rights, and you, as plaintiff, will have to allow these alternatives to take place. Some examples include:

Arbitration

Some written contracts require compulsory arbitration to be used to settle the matter. After the arbitration is completed, you could face an arbitrator's decision that is either adverse or that does not fully offer the compensation you feel is appropriate. Although the requirement for arbitration may be mandatory in some states, the decision can be appealed to any civil court. In most cases, small claims courts have the necessary jurisdiction to hear the complete case and maintain or reverse the ruling of the arbitrator in whole or in part. An adverse arbitrator's decision may become final after a short period, so you should be ready to file your court case when you start arbitration.

Countersuits and Counterclaims

The defendant has a right to countersue the plaintiff, claiming facts not within the scope of the plaintiff's suit against the defendant. A counterclaim can be made by the defendant to widen the issues the court must decide before emitting a judgment. A countersuit can claim damages that the plaintiff caused to the defendant. In most states, countersuits and counterclaims are incorporated into the original case, and then, it is tried as one case. This may make your job of proving your case more difficult, and the defense against the countersuits and counterclaims may bring forth evidence not previously part of the case.

Revisiting the Statute of Limitations

The statute of limitations is different for each type of case. The statute of limitations is also deemed to start at a certain time for each kind of dispute. In some states, there are several possible limits on the particular statute of limitations. For example, the start time in a contract dispute case may begin when the contract was signed, when the contract was set to end, at any time a dispute arose, or at a given time, such as a year after the contract signing. Check to be sure you have the correct rule established and are within the proper time.

SUMMARY

This chapter is designed to help you cross off item 17 of the Small Claims Checklist (**Figure 1.1**). It seems that no matter how well you plan a case initially, something changes after the court filing to alter the presentation of your case on the trial day. Some of the events and actions listed here will appear on the first scheduled trial date. These often result with the court setting a new trial date. The judge may direct you to complete certain tasks to have the case ready for this new date.

It is also possible that the defendant will have to follow orders of the court if he claims a legal error was made in your initial filing. For example, in cases where the defendant claims he or she was not legally served, the judge may tell the defendant that because he is present, he waives the plaintiff's error in serving the defendant in a timely fashion. It is also possible that any issues of the statute of limitations or venue will require affirmative evidence to be presented to extend the trial date until a future date.

Because small claims matters can always be appealed, the court can move forward to speedy justice in anticipation of preventing more work for the individuals and the court in the future. The best defense for the type of matters in this chapter is the development of the basic legal knowledge that you must comprehend to prevail in acting as your own attorney. Learn the terms in the Glossary of Legal Terms. If there is anything that you cannot understand, go to the library, look on the Internet, or ask your court clerk or legal adviser. These are all excellent sources that will motivate you in making a successful presentation.

CHAPTER 5:

SPECIAL SOLUTIONS FOR SPECIFIC CASES

TYPES OF CASES ALLOWED IN SMALL CLAIMS COURT

Many types of cases can be brought before a small claims court. Although none of the matters involved are criminal in nature, numerous types of civil court cases can be tried in small claims court if the state's monetary limits have not been exceeded. The most common cases are as follows:

Breach of Contract

There are two kinds of contract disputes. The first is called a non-participating contract dispute. This is most commonly called a debt collection action and will be further discussed later in this chapter. The second type of breach of contract is where both parties claim the other party has failed to meet his or her responsibilities under the contract. This is called a participating contract dispute. These cases can be taken to small claims court, and the judge will listen to both points of view, examine the evidence, and listen to any witnesses or expert testimony to determine which party is in default of one or more of the contract's term(s). In this type of case, the judge can use the Judgment of Solomon where Solomon was to cut a baby in half to determine the true mother. He can assign fault to both parties, then determine which party tends to be more at fault.

Participating contracts can be ruled invalid by the Statute of Frauds. All states have some sort of Statute of Frauds, which comes originally from English law. It means that certain types of contracts, as spelled out in your state's law, require that the agreement be set down in writing and signed by the party against whom the enforcement is sought. Note that this does not require both parties sign — only the party that is being asked to comply with the terms of the contract.

Property Damage

There are three major issues in property damage cases. The first is proof of the damage. In this situation, pictures and estimates by independent third parties are important. In some cases, repair costs may not be the only measure. For example, an automobile may not be worth as much as a used vehicle immediately after damage repair than it was right before the accident. People now can look at the vehicle damage report and devalue the car because it might not properly function in the future.

The second issue is fault. Take the case of a tree straddling a property line. If wind blows it on to either house, both property owners may be at fault, but not either's owner's insurance company. In most states, it is the property owner's responsibility to trim the tree or remove it if a hazard exists to either house.

The final issue is the value of the damaged item in the marketplace at the time of the accident. For example, the loss of a detached garage due to faulty wiring repair would be worth what other similarly situated and sized detached garages are worth. The real estate market changes with time, and the purchase price may have little to do with the value in the present market unless it was purchased recently.

Personal Injury

Not all states allow personal injury cases to be heard in small claims court. For those states that do allow it, you must carefully calculate the amount you seek. Often, these cases have so much money at stake that you would be wise to use an attorney and proceed with a suit in a higher civil court. Some insurance carriers and guarantors will offer mediation or arbitration, which may be as good as hiring an attorney, considering the attorney's fees involved.

The direct costs are your out-of-pocket medical costs, the medical costs paid by your insurance carrier, your lost pay (including lost vacation or accumulated personal days), and any durable medical equipment. You should have witnesses or written documentation that testifies what these costs were and how they have been calculated.

To document medical costs, bring your hospital and doctor bills and estimate mileage for travel to and from the doctors' offices in your private car. Also include any ambulance costs, medicine, medical supplies, or special medical equipment. If you have medical insurance, be sure that your policy has a clause for adding the amount the insurance paid, and reimburse it after any legal action. You can ask medical providers and hospitals to supply an itemized bill for all charges for use in the trial. If you have any doubt about acquiring the details you need, subpoena the office of the doctors or hospitals involved and personally procure the information.

You may recover all lost earnings, plus sick or vacation days, if those were indeed lost. This means that if your employer has an unlimited sick leave policy, you cannot collect on lost pay. If you were paid by your employer and did not suffer a loss of accumulated sick days, you cannot collect this in court.

In most civil cases, payments for pain and suffering are the largest part of the judgment. You will not find small claims cases with large judgments for pain and suffering. On average, what you will collect may be three to four times the actual medical costs. That is why it is important to get exact costs of all expenditures, including expenses accrued while traveling to doctors' offices for appointments. Make copies of all receipts.

Motor Vehicle Repair

The type of case referred to here is something called a botched auto repair case. The secret to winning this case is to make it easy for a non-mechanical-minded person to understand what happened, in plain and simple terms. To most people, the workings of an automobile are limited to such issues as turning the wheel to change direction, pushing the right pedal to go faster, or pushing the left pedal to slow or stop. The reason that an improper repair of a cylinder valve causes the car to throw a rod is beyond most jury members' or judges' knowledge. Do not assume they will know much about the auto repair business.

The same lack of knowledge may be present in your own mind when you start to prepare a case. Conversing for a few minutes with a local mechanic or a mechanically gifted friend may give you all the knowledge needed to explain what the mechanic did wrong in your botched repair job. You need to know the causes and be able to present them in simple terms.

The next issue is estimating the damage costs associated with the repair. First, there is a possibility that the defendant mechanic did work that — although repaired correctly — was not necessary or helpful in fixing the problem that brought your automobile to the shop in the first place. You may need an expert witness mechanic to sort out these costs so that you can seek a refund of monies that were nonessential.

If the repair caused further damage to your car, you will need to obtain an estimate of how much it will cost to return the car into working order. In our example, the costs are likely to be high; therefore, you should have three or more estimates. If the car has to be towed from mechanic to mechanic to get the estimates, these towing costs should be added to the bill. If you use an expert witness have the person point out the cause of the damage to the court and explain why all details of the estimate are necessary.

When you secure the estimates, make sure your expert has told you how the information should be presented. Do not start by suggesting that the estimate be for the lowest possible cost necessary to make your car run again. Recommend using new parts rather than refurbished parts. Also, suggest buying parts rather than having the repairs done by the mechanic in the auto shop. You are trying to build a case for enough money from the settlement to adequately repair the car. The judgment may not be for all work requested because the defendant may bring his or her own estimate of the costs to restore the vehicle to running order.

One last tip is to render a good drawing, which can contribute to your evidence. Try contacting your local high school's auto repair class teacher for pictures from textbooks, training manuals, or auto manufacturers' step-by-step diagnostic and repair guides. This person might even provide a hand-drawn explanation of the likely cause of the mechanic's faulty work.

Motor Vehicle Damage

In a case where auto damage is the result of an accident, the judge and jury do not have to understand the technical details of the repair — they only need to know the cost as shown in three or more estimates. Some insurance companies will provide an estimate from a claims adjustor at their selected repair facility. Unless the insurance company is declaring the vehicle a total loss, it is better to get independent estimates from actual repair shops.

Most motor vehicle damage cases that go to court are either cases where the defendant is uninsured or the plaintiff's insurance company's offer seems like an amount that is considerably lower than your expectations. When the defendant is insured and you are satisfied with your insurance company's compensation, there is no reason to take the matter to small claims court. If you are depending on the uninsured defendant to pay for your repairs, be sure that he or she has the assets and income to pay. The reason many people are uninsured is the cost. When such people imply it is a hardship to carry insurance, this is an obvious indication they have few assets.

The key to winning these types of cases is to determine that the defendant is at fault through his or her negligence. In most cases, negligence is legally determined by proving that the other driver caused the accident — in whole or in part — by failing to follow safety issues pertaining to the state's driving laws. The issue of cause is substantial. A case where a driver ran a traffic light is a violation of the laws in all states and is automatically established as a cause. However, a driver not wearing a seat belt violates a law, but it is not the cause of an accident.

It is important to report even minor accidents to law enforcement. The accident report and any citations for violating the law can be the difference in winning or losing a small claims case. In some cases, state law requires that vehicles remaining operable be driven to the nearest safe parking area. If you have a cell phone, call 911 and wait for the arrival of law enforcement. When the officer arrives and questions you, be sure to show him or her your position when the accident occurred and notify the officer of any apparent violations of safety laws by the other party. Most accident reports include a drawing of the collision with regard to other streets, driveways, and buildings. It is never a bad idea to make a similar drawing so that you can help explain your side of the mishap if you go to trial.

If your accident happened with a professional driver (truck driver, taxi, delivery van), it is important to have the documentation or witnesses that will show the probable fault. It is a good idea to keep a small disposable camera in your car's glove compartment for taking pictures of the accident site, the view from your initial position, the defendant's view from his position, and the final resting area. If you do not have a disposable camera, use the camera in your cell phone to document as much of the "before" and "after" situations as you can. Although judges know that professional drivers often feel it necessary to protect their driving records by testifying about the ingrained safety routines at such critical times as traffic lights, corners, and small spaces, you should expect to defend your position in your questioning of the defendant.

New Vehicle Purchases

Most states have what are called "lemon laws" that supplement your rights over the manufacturer's limited warranty. The typical law covers defects found in either the first 18,000 miles or 18 months of ownership. There have been many cases where the defects were denied by the manufacturers for years only to be found after the lemon law expired.

There was a publicized case with Volkswagen®, where its pop-top camper vans had a defect in the air conditioner, which failed in such a catastrophic manner that the engine stalled from the stress brought on by the air conditioner. The condition disabled vehicles in areas of extreme heat, such as desert climates. After a major class action suit, it was later found that the cause was a missing part that cost less than a dollar. The fact most disturbing to consumers was the idea that the German company's main office knew about the problem within three months of the first discovery. In most cases, the value of the vehicle is too high for lemon law relief as a small claims court matter.

If you want to get repairs that are under warranty and the dealer refuses to repair it without cost, you have the right to sue for those costs in small claims court. Be sure to have the warranty reviewed by a legal advisor before starting the action, as warranties are often complicated and hard to interpret. If you are having difficulty getting an item fixed, notwithstanding its coverage under the warranty, document your efforts with receipts and outside evaluations of your problem.

Popular vehicles with known problems are documented on the federal government Web site at **www.nhtsa.dot.gov**. If you find your predicament listed there, mention to the dealer that the problem is being documented by the National Highway Traffic Safety Administration. If the dealer does not respond by making the necessary fixes, take the dealership to court. The Web site also documents company service bulletins that may represent a secret warranty or special issue that the manufacturer does not want brought up in the courts.

Used Vehicle Purchases from Dealers

Purchases from used car dealers are tricky to resolve in small claims court. Many cars sold from these dealers are sold "without warranty" or "as is." Your best chance of getting a used car dealer to repair problems on your vehicle is to potentially damage the dealership's reputation by having a case appear in court.

You should reread the sales contract that you signed when purchasing the car and determine if there are any differences from the verbal representations the dealer made and what is in the contract. It is a good idea to have a friend with you when buying a used vehicle. As a buyer, one never knows when you may need a witness to collaborate how the vehicle was verbally represented.

There are two key elements to winning this type of case. First, it necessitates proof of loss due to the car. If you have paid the repair costs and the vehicle now works, you can justify the first required element. The second element, which is harder to prove, is presenting authentication that the dealer is legally responsible for the damages. If your dealer misrepresented the car and you have a witness to this, you can prove that the dealer is responsible. The dealer will likely say something like, "It is a 10-year-old vehicle. I had no way of knowing about the problem." He may also point to statements in the sales contract that state no written or oral statements by the salesperson, other than the sales contract, shall be considered representations of the quality of the vehicle.

Your best argument in casting fault against the dealer is to argue fraud. Try to prove the exact comments that the dealer or salesperson made when representing the auto at the time. Make sure you quote any statements that you feel were an "expressed" or "implied" warranty. The best proof is a witness with you at the time of purchase. Remember to keep a folder with any copies of ads, fliers, or other written descriptions of the vehicle. These aid in the establishment of an implied warranty and help refresh your recollection of the conversations.

You may find evidence of fraud in the vehicle itself. When you ask an expert mechanic to diagnose the problem, inquire as to why the trouble did not appear at the time you took the test drive and listened to the engine running. You may find that the outside mechanic knows which trick was used to mask symptoms of the problems you later found. Often, special oils or fluids can be treated with a foreign compound to make the car appear free of defect for a short time.

You can also argue an implied warranty. For example, if you go on to the lot with a friend and ask for a car that would be a "reliable, going-to-work car" and the dealer directs you to certain cars, these cars are considered "implied" to be suitably reliable as a vehicle for daily transportation. When the car has to spend time in the shop, forcing you to either seek a different means to get to work or perhaps miss work, you have proven that the car was not the type of automobile you expressly requested.

Used Vehicle Purchased from a Private Party

Getting redress from small claims court for a vehicle purchased from a private individual is often easier than from a dealer. Although you have all the options outlined in the previous section, additional solutions also may be available. First, the defendant is not likely to be as legally sophisticated as a commercial used car dealer. In most cases, these private-party sales do not involve a sales contract. Most likely, the only signed document in the transaction will be the transfer of title.

The major issue with this type of transaction is the same as with the purchase of a car from a used car dealer. You need to prove that the car was represented one way and that later repair costs showed quite a different outcome. Just like the dealer case, a witness to the presentation of the car and the original ad may be important in convincing the judge that you are the wronged party and the defendant is at fault.

Defective Product

If you or your property were injured or damaged by a defective product, you will likely qualify to recover your costs under the legal doctrine of strict liability. This type of law holds that the manufacturer is responsible for damages suffered by a buyer without having to prove negligence. For example, if a can of spray paint produces a poor color and destroys the surface onto which it was sprayed, you can recover the cost of replacing or repainting the item without proving the manufacturer or seller was negligent.

In this type of case, the key is to document damages through pictures, witnesses, or other evidence. Keep accounts of all costs associated with the restoration of the damaged item. You should also have proof of purchase of the defective item to verify that you are not guilty under the "clean hands doctrine." For example, if you had shoplifted the spray paint from the retail outlet, you cannot sue because you were guilty of a different legal issue in the same transaction.

Breach of Warranty

There are several types of warranties. These are all part of a landmark warranty case started in Kansas and, ultimately, became United States law by a Supreme Court decision. The resulting doctrine was codified into the Magnuson-Moss Warranty Federal Trade Commission Improvements Act. The following types of warranties flow from this law into all state courts:

- **Expressed written warranty**: If a product comes with a written warranty, the buyer has a right to expect the product to operate as represented, even if it was a limited warranty. You can rely on the seller's description of the product and its functionality, as well as on any promise of the product being free of defects. If the product has an express warranty to maintain performance of the product, it should not require repair, replacement of defective parts, or exchange for a reconditioned unit.

- **Express oral warranties**: If the seller makes a specific oral statement while selling the product, such as, "The brake pads on this sports edition will last you 25,000 miles under all conditions," you have a right to be compensated if this warranty statement becomes untrue in the future. This oral warranty is valid, even if the brake manufacturer's warranty says that the brakes are warranted for only 20,000 miles. When going to court, you must be able to prove the seller made the oral warranty. Otherwise, the written warranty will apply.

- **Implied warranties**: Most retail products are designed for an ordinary purpose, such as a DVD player being suitable for reading professionally prerecorded DVDs and outputting the signal to a television set. This is an implied warranty, which exists in addition to any expressed written or oral warranties about the product's maintenance or performance.

To bring a breach of warranty case before most small claims courts, you need to have notified only the manufacturer about the problem and given it a reasonable time to remedy the situation. The court will not normally consider relief to you under a warranty issue unless you have made a good-faith effort to give the seller or manufacturer a chance to remedy the situation.

Dog Bite

Most cases involving dogs are dog bite cases. In most states, the owner is liable for injuries caused by the dogs (or other pets). Many states do not consider dog behavior the responsibility of owners. In some areas, where rural nomad dogs roam from farm to farm, feeding on the handouts of the community, a dog may not be considered the property of anyone. The injuries from a dog bite must occur on the property of the owner. In some states, injuries from a dog other than those caused by a bite, such as scratches or injuries due to a dog jumping up on a person, are not covered.

If you wish to file a dog bite case, check the law in your state. If there is no law, your state legislative body may have left the matter to "common law." This legal concept forces the plaintiff to prove that the defendant knew of the dog's viciousness or should have been aware of it before the owner can be sanctioned. Common law dog bite cases are hard to prove.

In cases where you have to rely on common law, you might consider an anti-barking law if one exists in the municipality where you live. You can use the noise of the dog as a nuisance that needs to be abated and obtain damages if you prove the nuisance. Suits regarding pets often place neighbor against neighbor and may even put groups of the neighborhood against others in the community. To resolve the issues in a friendly fashion, you might consider mediation rather than a lawsuit.

Withholding Rent

Withholding rent is an action that a renter starts against the landlord over repairs that have not been done to maintain a rental unit's habitability. For a tenant to prove the right to be allowed to withhold rent, the person must not have caused the problem. The defect must be serious enough to threaten the tenant's health and safety, and the landlord must have been given reasonable notice of existence of the condition.

Withholding rent is not considered reasonable if the landlord is merely slow to fix problems, whether the speed of repairs is for a specific case or as a rule. The withholding must be a single major health hazard or a group of smaller hazards that, when taken together, constitute a condition of being uninhabitable.

For a landlord to bring a suit to stop a tenant from withholding rent, he needs to prove only that the stated, such as water not being hot enough, has either been repaired or was not a serious health hazard, as attested to by a certified professional who normally services the hot water of the building.

If the defect claimed is substantial, the notice of the problem must have been timely enough to allow the landlord to evaluate the problem, seek competent professionals to do the work, and allow time for the work to be done. Withholding rent ahead of this rather long and involved process will likely be deemed illegal.

A defect that is small and allowed to remain for an unreasonably long time may not be sustained to the full amount of the rent if the tenant was simply inconvenienced by the problem or had to spend what amounted to a small portion of the rent to resolve the problem. For example, if the air conditioning does not blow enough cool air into the bedroom to allow the tenant to sleep, and the tenant can remedy this by the purchase of a $15 fan to blow the cool air from other rooms into the bedroom, the tenant can win only the $15 he spent for the fan.

Landlord-Tenant Cases

There are numerous types of landlord-tenant disputes, and many end up in small claims court. For easy discussion, a few are broken down into the following categories:

- **Secure housing issues**: The tenant has a right to secure housing. This includes the right to be free from assailants, drug pushers, and thieves. If a tenant can prove a loss has occurred due to one of these acts and the landlord has not made a reasonable attempt to prevent this crime, the loss can be brought to the landlord. If the landlord was not notified of the potential danger or given sufficient time to take reasonable measures to eliminate or reduce the insecurity, it is unlikely that the court would award damages. The primary provider of safe and secure living is the law enforcement branch of government. There are limits on what the landlord can do to secure a rental. These measures are largely limited to securing windows and doors, safety lighting outside the rental unit, and, if necessary, putting up fencing to prevent access to the property.

- **Issues of discrimination**: It is illegal to discriminate against a potential tenant based solely on the basis of children in the family, race, age, nationality, sex, sexual orientation, disability, or the renter's receiving public assistance. This discrimination extends to the reasons for eviction or changes in the conditions of the lease. Although decisive discrimination cases are rarely brought to small claims court due to the monetary limits, the courts can assert jurisdiction. The rules of law and proof points for discrimination are large enough to be a subject of a book itself. The key is that the causes have difficult evidence issues and are likely best brought by a civil authority that can represent a group of tenants that has been discriminated against by the particular landlord.

- **Issues of habitable conditions and fitness of purpose**: A tenant can seek remedies in small claims court in place of such things as withholding rent to get the landlord to fix long-term issues of health and safety. It should be noted that commercial leases normally do not require habitability or suitability of purpose. For example, if a commercial junkyard operator leased a piece of property on a long-term basis without getting the necessary required permits and zoning issues, it is not the landlord's responsibility to obtain them for the tenant or prove that the property is fit for a particular commercial purpose.

- **On-premise crime and drug issues**: The landlord may rent to a drug dealer or perpetrator of a crime that will degrade the neighborhood without knowing of this person's actions in advance. Moreover, when the landlord finds out what is going on within the rental, he or she must take all reasonable steps to evict the tenants. Drug manufacturers, such as those making methamphetamine, create an additional safety hazard to the neighborhood. In these cases, the premises may be so contaminated that the unit and surrounding units have to be decontaminated or torn down to remove the safety hazard. Although these situations are unlikely cases for small claims court due to the monetary limits various states impose, the court could order the necessary demolition as part of any monetary judgment.

- **Issues of late payment of rent and eviction**: The landlord has a right to receive timely rent for any residential, industrial, or commercial units he or she rents. When rent is late beyond any grace period granted in the lease or verbal contract between the landlord and tenant, the landlord can go to court to receive rent and evict the tenant from the unit. This type of case, quite common in small claims court, is called an unlawful detainer case. Some landlords will avoid small claims court with these types of cases because it often takes longer to get the tenants out of the unit. Often-evicted tenants quickly learn they can request extensions of time on the initial trial date and will appeal the decision, effectively living rent-free for several months in the landlord's property.

- **Issues of landlord entry and the "obnoxious landlord:"** Some landlords spend too much time at the rentals making repairs or checking to see if things are all right. The landlord's presence can even turn into such issues as sexual harassment. One major issue between tenants and landlords revolves around access to the inside of a unit. Tenants feel they have an absolute right to privacy, and this is true in most cases. The laws vary from state to state, but the landlord often has a right to enter the premises for emergencies, to make required repairs, to show the property when the current tenant is leaving, and when the tenant gives specific permission. If the landlord does not follow the law and is habitually an "obnoxious landlord," this may be a case for small claims court. The courts of many states will award monetary damages for intentional infliction of emotional distress.

Professional Malpractice

Professional malpractice requires four conditions to be met before there is an actionable case to file in a court. First, it must be a legal and well-defined duty a professional must perform as part of his or her work. A day laborer who works a series of unskilled jobs on a day-by-day basis would not have a set of standard professional duties, so he could not be sued for malpractice. Doctors, lawyers, and dentists, on the other hand, have a highly defined level of duty associated with their professions. There are skilled professions that may not meet the requirement of duty for malpractice cases. For example, a beautician who dyes your hair may have a responsibility to eliminate any hint of gray that makes you look older; however, his or her failure to do this may not be malpractice.

The second requirement of malpractice is causation. You must be able to prove that the professional's conduct was the one and only cause of the problem for which you seek compensation. The definition of causation is limited. You must effectively prove that the professional you are suing made an error that other similarly trained professionals would not make under the exact circumstances. You may need an expert witness of the same profession to testify to the causation issue.

Third, you must prove that the professional was careless. A professional who fails to use the normal and customary tools and methods to do the job that others in his or her specialty would use may be deemed legally careless. Again, you may need a professional to identify the fault in the professional's reasoning or technique that caused the malpractice.

Finally, you must substantiate the damages that you have suffered, or may suffer in the future, that are a direct result of this instance of malpractice. For example, suppose a dentist suggests that he will have to repair a particular tooth at your next visit; however, he repairs a different tooth at the appointment. You later find the tooth has decayed to the point that it is not savable, requiring that a bridge be made. You may be compensated for your pain and suffering, the additional cost of a second repair, and such indirect costs as the lack of a professional appearance by the loss of your perfect smile.

Nuisance

Legal cases can arise out of concepts of either private nuisance or public nuisance. Whenever someone hinders your ability to enjoy the benefits of your real or personal property, it is categorized as a private nuisance. One example might be frequent outside parties with loud music in your neighbor's backyard. Another example would be a person who has chained dogs that circle and growl whenever you go out your front door. Either of these is considered a nuisance. You are due monetary damage if you can prove certain conditions exist, as follows:

- You own or rent the property in question.

- The defendant created the condition or maintained a nuisance that was harmful to your health, or the condition was indecent, offensive, or obstructed you from the free use of your property. You must not have given the person your permission to engage in the conduct that interferes with your enjoyment or use of the property. A reasonable person would deem the conduct annoying or disturbing. If you can prove you were harmed by the conduct, the continued public benefits, if any, are outweighed by an existence of a private nuisance's benefit.

A public nuisance is different from its private cousin. In this case, the nuisance in question affects the health and safety of the public or at least a group of people. The change of an aircraft beacon that routes air traffic over your neighborhood at night at low altitude may constitute a public nuisance. Public nuisance suits are rarely filed in small claims court because of the monetary limits that states impose on small claims cases. Public nuisance claims are often the measuring of a balance between public benefit and public nuisance of a particular phenomenon.

Bad Check, Non-Participating Contract Disputes, and Bad Debt

The bad debt type of suit centers on the efforts of a plaintiff to collect a debt created by some action in the past. The first example is a bad check. A check returned to the payee due to lack of funds in the account is a bad check. It can be collected by court action and does not necessitate proving the debt that the check had intended to satisfy.

A non-participating contract dispute is a debt in which neither party disputes the underlying need for payment. An example would be if a plumber does some work on a new house for the general contractor building a "spec" house and is not paid. In many cases, neither the contractor nor subcontracting plumber dispute the work was done and that payment is due. It may be some other party, such as the speculator financing the construction of the house, who is at fault in the unpaid debt.

Bad debt is a term encompassing all other kinds of debt that may be brought before the small claims court. For example, this could be a florist suing the estate of a deceased individual by way of the estate's executor for flowers used on a casket during the family viewing and burial proceeding. (In a few cases, estate debt has to go before the probate court.) Any kind of debt where a good or service was not paid for after being ordered and delivered is a bad debt and collectible in court.

Libel, Slander, and Defamation

To prove libel, slander, or defamation of character, you need to prove that the other party wrote or said something that is untrue about you or your business. Simple freedom of speech in expressing an opinion is not enough to go to court. Also, if you are a public person, such as an actor or other celebrity, you may not be able to sue under these statutes in some states. To obtain damages for any proven libel, slander, or defamation of character, you must prove the action truly damaged your stature or reputation. You must also prove that the other person's acts against you were in "reckless disregard" of the truth.

Cases Involving Minors

You can sue a minor only by suing the minor's parents, legal guardian, or guardian ad litem. Because minors are not considered emancipated persons until a certain age in each state, they are not able to enter into contracts, whether written, oral, or implied. Minors are unlikely to have funds available to pay damages. The only effective way to sue a minor for damages would be to sue the minor and the parents.

In most states, neither the minor nor the parents can be held responsible for the minor's negligence. The theory of the guarded status of a minor is that he or she is too young to make sound decisions or to act in a rational manner. The principal exception to the minor's inability to be sued is called "malicious and willful misconduct." The parent is supposed to teach the minor not to act in an irresponsible manner and, therefore, the parent can be held financially responsible for damages that arise out of the malicious and willful misconduct of the minor.

Clothing and Other Favorite Items

When you visit small claims court to see what it is like, you will notice how many people are suing over a piece of clothing mangled by a dry cleaner or a cheap watch ruined by a merchant trying to replace its dead battery. Many customers of small businesses get upset about the loss of their cherished items. The best you can hope to receive as compensation for these items is the fair market value as a used item in an establishment specializing in the sale of used goods. A favorite sweater or discount branded watch, even with ironclad at-fault issues, is worth only a few dollars. Often, your time is not worth a small claims case in such instances.

Police Brutality/False Arrest Cases

If an attorney refuses your police brutality case or false arrest case, you can take it to small claims court. When appearing there, you will likely find out the reason that the attorney refused to represent you. The truth is that attacks on the "thin blue line" are seldom worth the effort. The police may stand in unison against you. It will also be likely that you cannot, and you may not, find a witness who will help in proving unjust treatment.

Most law enforcement personnel realize that a single black mark on their records can affect their promotions and, ultimately, their pensions. If you were manhandled or arrested without the smallest hint of evidence, you should trust the advice of an attorney, who would make a handsome fee and nice public record if he or she could win your case. If someone turns it down, it is best to give up.

Internet Purchases

Internet purchases are on the frontier of small claims court law. In most cases, when you do business with an Internet merchant, the seller resides and has its business headquarters in a state other than where you live. You can find out who owns the business site you use at **www. networksolutions.com/whois/index.jsp**. This site provides information that tells you in which state the server is located and in what state the owner does business. It will also show its address, which is sometimes difficult to access.

If the Internet business (or its server site) you choose to take to small claims court is headquartered in your state, you can easily file the suit there. If the business is located out of state, you may still be able to sue it in your state. The court will let you sue it through its out-of-state address only if you can prove one of the following:

- The company regularly does business in your state. You may know this if someone local recommended the Web site for a particular type of merchandise.

- If the company has dealers in your state, check its Web site for authorized dealers.

- If the company has agents, plants, distributors, warehouses, or other affiliates in your state that you can locate through phone directories or Web searches, you can also sue it in its home state.

Otherwise, you will find most small claims courts will not allow you to sue an out-of-state firm, due to the extreme cost on the defendant that such a case would cause.

SPECIAL COURTS

Divorce Court without an Attorney

Most divorce proceedings are handled in family court, not in small claims court. However, in either case, you can represent yourself on a pro se basis if the other party also represents him or herself. Every state allows some kind of no-fault divorce. The major issues in a divorce are the division of the property jointly owned, the custody of any minor children, the visitation rights of either noncustodial parent, and spousal and child support. Both parties to the divorce should seriously consider all the issues and their lifetime implications before going to court for a fast pro per divorce decree.

CHAPTER 6:

BANKRUPTCY (341A HEARING, REPRESENTATION FOR YOURSELF)

Debtors filing for bankruptcy under Chapter 7 of the current bankruptcy law may represent themselves at the Meeting of Creditors, or 341(a) hearing, established under 11 USC Section 521 of the United States Code. Here, the appointed bankruptcy trustee and the creditors question the debtor as to the location and value of assets that the debtor may possess. The debtor can make decisions with respect to secured debt and the decision to put all or part of the debt of it on the statement of intention.

The federal distinction between what is secured property and what is unsecured property was changed by recent revisions to the law. You will find that it is extremely detailed in its analysis. Any debtor representing himself pro se in this hearing should understand the asset definition difference so that the correct long-term decision can be made. The new revisions to the law lengthen the time after one bankruptcy before a debtor can file a new bankruptcy.

OFF-LIMIT CASES

Out-of-State Defendant Cases

You cannot sue an out-of-state resident in your state's small claims court. Most states' judges know it is costly for defendants to travel a good distance to defend themselves. There are several notable exceptions:

- An out-of-state business can be sued if it has an office or authorized agent located within your state where you can serve the court papers.

- Out-of-state residents whom you manage to serve while they are staying in or passing through your state.

- Nonresidents who have had a vehicular accident in your state. You may sue either the owner of the vehicle or the driver of the vehicle, if they are different, when the accident was in the court's jurisdiction.

- Out-of-state residents who own real property in your state.

- A business with a breach of contract suit can file the case in the state where the contract was negotiated or performed, even if the contracting business is based outside your state.

- The business has an office, warehouse, retail establishment, restaurant, or other physical facility in your state.

- A company that sells products within the state by employing sales reps who can be personally served.

Cases Against Prisoners and Military Personnel

In most instances, prisoners and military personnel on active duty cannot be sued. Military personnel can agree to be sued if they either have a supervisor's approval to appear on the trial date, or it is agreed by the plaintiff, defendant, and the court that the issue will be resolved through the exchange of documents and letters.

SUMMARY

This chapter dealt with specific evidence, rules, laws, and restrictions that may be involved with certain types of cases. These types of cases can overlap, or maybe your particular case has more than one aspect. If you read the chapter, you may be able to consolidate your facts and present a better case that will improve your chances of winning the maximum amount of your loss. On the other hand, if your case is constrained by the state maximum, you win only the state-mandated limit.

CHAPTER 7:

GETTING ORGANIZED FOR SMALL CLAIMS COURT

The small claims courts across the country differ from each other. In larger cities, there will likely be a judge in a courtroom with tables for the plaintiff and defendants. There is often a gallery where witnesses and other interested persons can sit to watch the proceeding or await their call before the judge. In more rural areas, you may find a schoolteacher or an appointed official sitting as a judge in a classroom of the high school, deciding the cases on his or her interpretation of the law.

Some states have developed their small claims systems to the point of having special rooms that look less like courtrooms and more like conference rooms with galleries. Some small claims courts have rooms for mediators to meet with the parties coming before the court in the hope of finding a mutually agreeable solution before it has to go before the judge.

WHERE IS THE COURT?

Before you consider filing a small claims court case, you need to locate the court where the case will be tried. In some states, that will be in the county seat. Depending on the rules of your state, the court may be in another county that is nearby your residence and the home of the defendant or defendant's business that you plan to sue. In a few cases, such as in the largest county in the United States, San Bernardino County, Calif., the court could be more than a hundred miles away but still be in your county of residence.

Check the Web, call the court clerk's office, or visit the court yourself to locate any necessary forms and obtain a fee schedule. If the fees are higher than you can comfortably pay, ask if there is a procedure to have the fees waived or become due only with the satisfaction of the court's judgment against the defendant. Ask the court clerk about any available legal advice service. Some clerks will provide a law student who is assisting in the clerk's office, and others will recommend another office nearby.

The first issue to establish with the clerk's office is that of venue. Explain enough of your lawsuit to the clerk to get his or her advice on whether the court has venue. If the other party is a resident of another county or has his or her only business location in another county, you may have to go to that county to find venue for the suit. Because each state is different, check Appendix B.

Ask the court clerk about the normal trial times you could expect for your trial date when it is scheduled. In some jurisdictions, you may have a choice of a morning, afternoon, or evening session. The clerk will likely quote a time, such as 9 a.m. on each Tuesday and Thursday of the week. This does not mean your case will be heard at exactly 9 a.m. on a particular date. The court session will likely have several cases on the calendar and, therefore, will assign the order in which cases are heard.

In many cases, it is important to be at the court a little before the time scheduled for your trial. You may find the courtroom number has been changed or that you are first directed to a mediation session before the actual trial. In some cases, the judge may take roll to determine if the defendants and plaintiffs are present for each case. Often, in cases where one of the parties is not there, the judge will take the case in his or her first group of cases for disposition. Cases where the plaintiff is absent will be dismissed, and that plaintiff will have to start the process over. In cases where the defendant is missing, often a default judgment is issued in the plaintiff's favor. If the defendant later appears, the default judgment can be set aside and a new trial date set.

In all cases, the judge will examine the timeliness of service on the defendant. If the defendant complains that he was not served within the required limits before the trial date, the court will reset the trial date. If the defendant argues issues of venue, the judge will rule on this matter before any other in the case. If the defendant argues the matter is not timely, the judge will examine the dates in relation to the statute of limitations for this type of case.

WHO IS THE DEFENDANT?

In most cases, it is the defendant's circumstances that will determine venue. For example, nonresidents of your county involved in an automobile accident within your county may be enough to establish venue. The defendant's auto insurance company may have an office in your county, and this may establish venue. Ask for advice if you are not sure about this legal concept.

You will also have to find an address to file service on the defendant. You need to determine where the person lives or the location of his or her business. If you find the defendant has moved, go to your post office and ask for assistance in getting the new forwarding address. The post office normally forwards any mail sent to an old address for the first six months after a person moves. However, you can ask that any mail be returned to you with the corrected address printed on the letter.

THE COURT PAPERWORK

The first paperwork the small claims court will require is the claim or filing. This identifies the plaintiff(s), defendant(s), and the cause for the hearing. Depending on the type of lawsuit filed, you may have to file papers with answers to different questions than in your initial filing. The other documents you need to file with the court will bring evidence and witnesses to support your case.

The following is a facsimile of a California form that is typical of the subpoenas you will need to use to have witnesses appear and have people not part of the lawsuit bring evidence you think is favorable to your case. If you are aware of evidence that the other party does not know about, ask your legal advisor if you have to notify the defendant of its existence in case he wants to use it in the case for his own purposes. Failure to do so in some states may be all it takes to void your favorable judgment.

The example is for a case where two neighbors are parties to the case of a dog bite. A third neighbor was a witness to the event and has pictures that show the bite incident and the resulting wounds. The subpoena is designed to be sure the neighbor with the proof appears as a witness and brings the pictures. If you read the whole document, you will see that the form also can be used for witnesses even if they do not have evidence to present.

Many of the universal forms that states use for small claims court will have a front and back side, so be sure to complete both sides and get the necessary signatures and seals. Sometimes there are portions of the form that you will not need to fill out. The court clerk's office can often explain how a form can be used and what part of the form is necessary for your purpose.

FIGURE 7.1: WITNESS SUBPOENA WITH REQUESTED EVIDENCE (FRONT)	
Name and Address of Court: Municipal Court San Bernardino County 44191 Sage Highway, Joshua Tree, CA XXXXX	Small Claims Case Number: JT1210-1221
PLAINTIFF 1: John Smith 123 Main Street Desert View, CA XXXXX	DEFENDANT 1: Mary Doe 125 Main Street Desert View, CA XXXXX

FIGURE 7.1: WITNESS SUBPOENA WITH REQUESTED EVIDENCE (FRONT)

Telephone Number: Telephone Number:

PLAINTIFF 2:   DEFENDANT 2:

None   None

Telephone Number: Telephone Number:

FORM 202D: SMALL CLAIMS COURT SUBPOENA

FOR PERSONAL APPEARANCE AND PRODUCTION OF DOCUMENTS

AND THINGS AT TRIAL OR HEARING AND CLARIFICATION

THE PEOPLE OF THE STATE OF CALIFORNIA, TO:

Marcellas Manito, 120 Main Street, Desert View, CA XXXXX

1. YOU ARE HEREBY ORDERED TO APPEAR AS A WITNESS in the case at the date, time, and place shown in the box below UNLESS your appearance is excused as indicated in box 4b or you make an agreement with the person named in Item 2. BELOW:

Date:	Time:	Dept.:	Div.:	Room:
June 12, 20XX	9 a.m.	189	DV	102

a.   Address:

44191 Sage Highway, Joshua Tree, CA XXXXX

2. IF YOU HAVE ANY QUESTIONS ABOUT THE TIME OR DATE YOU ARE TO APPEAR, OR IF YOU WANT TO BE CERTAIN THAT YOUR PRESENCE IS REQUIRED, CONTACT THE FOLLOWING PERSON BEFORE THE DATE ON WHICH YOU ARE TO APPEAR:

a. Name of Subpoenaing Party: Telephone:

John Smith   (XXX) XXX-XXXX

FIGURE 7.1: WITNESS SUBPOENA WITH REQUESTED EVIDENCE (FRONT)

3. Witness Fee: You are entitled to witness fees and mileage traveled both ways, as provided by law, if you request them at the time of service. You may request them before your scheduled appearance from the person named in Item 2.

4. YOU ARE:

a. ☑Ordered to appear in person and to produce the records in the declaration on page 2 (back). The personal attendance of the custodian, or other qualified witness, and the production of the original records are required by this subpoena. The procedure authorized by Evidence Code Section 21(b) is to be followed in compliance with this subpoena.

b. ☐Not required to appear in person if you produce the records described on page 2 (back) of this subpoena.

5. IF YOU HAVE BEEN SERVED WITH THIS SUBPOENA AS A CUSTODIAN OF CONSUMER OR EMPLOYEE RECORDS UNDER THE CIVIL CODE PROCEDURES AND A MOTION TO QUASH, OR AN OBJECTION HAS BEEN SERVED ON YOU, A COURT ORDER OR AGREEMENT OF THE PARTIES, WITNESSES AND CONSUMER EMPLOYEES AFFECTED MUST BE OBTAINED BEFORE YOU ARE REQUIRED TO PRODUCE CONSUMER OR EMPLOYEE RECORDS.

DISOBEDIENCE OF THIS SUBPOENA MAY BE PUNISHED AS CONTEMPT BY THIS COURT. YOU MAY ALSO BE LIABLE FOR THE SUM OF FIVE HUNDRED DOLLARS AND ALL DAMAGES RESULTING FROM YOUR FAILURE TO OBEY.

Date Issued: Justice Adderly Clerk, by   *Karen Millard*

FIGURE 7.2: WITNESS SUBPOENA WITH REQUESTED EVIDENCE (BACK)

Name and Address of Court:	Small Claims Case Number:
Municipal Court San Bernardino County	JT1210-1221
44191 Sage Highway, Joshua Tree, CA XXXXX	

DECLARATION IN SUPPORT OF

FORM 202D: SMALL CLAIMS COURT SUBPOENA

FIGURE 7.2: WITNESS SUBPOENA WITH REQUESTED EVIDENCE (BACK)

FOR PERSONAL APPEARANCE AND PRODUCTION OF DOCUMENTS

AND THINGS AT TRIAL OR HEARING AND CLARIFICATION

1. I, the undersigned, declare I am the ☑plaintiff ☐defendant ☐judgment creditor.

2. The witness has possession or control of the following documents or other things and shall produce them at the time and place specified on the Small Claims Court Subpoena on the first page (front) of this form.

Witnessed a dog bite on May 22, 20XX at 123 Main Street

a. ☐Continued of attachment 2a.

b. ☐ After trial to enforce a judgment:

(1) ☐ Payroll receipts, stubs, and other records concerning employment of the defendant party.

(2) ☐ Bank accounts, canceled checks and other records of the defendant's bank account.

(3) ☐ Savings account statements or passbooks of the defendant party.

(4) ☐ Stock certificates belonging or registered to the defendant.

(5) ☐ Automobile registration certificates or proof of ownership for the defendant party's vehicles.

(6) ☐ Any deeds or other records of ownership of real property in the name of the defendant.

(7) ☑Other (specify):

Photos you took for the incident and injury

3. __ Good cause exists for the production of the documents or other things in paragraph two for the following reasons:

FIGURE 7.2: WITNESS SUBPOENA WITH REQUESTED EVIDENCE (BACK)

Continued of attachment 3a.

Continued of attachment 3a.

4. __ These documents are material to issues in this case for the following reasons:

Continued of attachment 2a.

I declare under penalty of perjury under the laws of this state that the foregoing is true and correct.

Date Issued: May 20, 20XX Plaintiff _____ *John Smith* _____

FIGURE 7.3: PROOF OF SERVICE OF SMALL CLAIMS DOCUMENT

Proof of Service

Municipal Court San Bernardino County   JT1210-1221

Name and Address of Court: Small Claims Case Number:

44191 Sage Highway, Joshua Tree, CA XXXXX

PROOF OF SERVICE FOR
SMALL CLAIMS COURT SUBPOENA
FOR PERSONAL APPEARANCE AND PRODUCTION OF DOCUMENTS
AND THINGS AT TRIAL OR HEARING AND CLARIFICATION

IN THE MATTER OF THE PEOPLE OF THE STATE OF CALIFORNIA, TO:

Marcellas Manito, 120 Main Street, Desert View, CA XXXXX

FOR SERVICE TO APPEAR AS A WITNESS in the case at the date, time, and place shown in the box below UNLESS I DO CERTIFY THAT THE SERVICE HAS BEEN ACCOMPLISHED AS REQUIRED BY LAW FOR COURT ON THE DATE AND TIME. BELOW:

FIGURE 7.3: PROOF OF SERVICE OF SMALL CLAIMS DOCUMENT

Date:	Time:	Dept.:	Div.:	Room:
June 12, 20XX	9 a.m.	189	DV	102

Address:

44191 Sage Highway, Joshua Tree, CA XXXXX

1. Date of delivery:

    May 23, 20XX

2. Time of delivery:

    11:53 a.m.

3. Witness fee (check one)

    a. ☐were demanded and paid in the amount of $_____

    b. ☑were not demanded or paid.

4. Person serving is qualified under the law as follows:

    (1) ☐A registered California process server.

    (2) ☐A California sheriff, marshal, or constable.

    (3) ☐Not a registered California Process server.

    (4) ☐Employee or independent contractor of a registered California process server.

    (5) ☐Exempt from registration under Professions Code 2250(b).

    (6) ☐Registered professional photocopier.

    (7) ☑Exempt from registration under Professions Code 22451.

FIGURE 7.3: PROOF OF SERVICE OF SMALL CLAIMS DOCUMENT

5. Server's address, including phone, and registration numbers, if applicable:

Harry Wells, Coster Paralegal, 711 Court House Court, Joshua Tree, CA Phone (XXX) XXX-XXXX Registration not required.

I declare under penalty of perjury under the laws of this state that the document enumerated herein has been served on the individual required.

Harry Wells

Date Issued: May 23, 20XX Service Official

Most forms that the court requires will have to be served on the defendant, witness, or person holding evidence. You will find that the means of service varies from state to state and area to area within a state. It is sometimes a court official such as a marshal, or someone from the sheriff's office. Quite often, the law says that the person who serves the document of the court must be a person not involved in the case.

As you can see, the state of California has several private party or businesses that may be used to serve paperwork of the small claims court on the defendant or witness. The court clerk should know if this type of private service is available and legal in your state. A phone call to some of the various types of services recommended will give you information on their costs and guarantees. You want to be sure your defendants and witnesses are properly served so that you can win the case.

It is not recommended that you use a service that ultimately relies on a registered letter. Most people refuse to accept them or wait until the last day to sign for them. A late signing date will result in an automatic request for a new trial date, because the defendant or witness did not receive it in time. If you have expert witnesses or friends coming as your witnesses, you will find this can cost you money and good feelings. A case that does not come together at the trial date can be disastrous to the final outcome.

If you will be using devices such as video players or slide projectors, ask the court clerk if they are available. You may have to bring your own, but sometimes they are available if you arrange for this in advance by filing the necessary special forms clerks have for this purpose.

In most jurisdictions, it is not necessary to provide evidence or special documentation for the judge at the time of filing. However, there are a few states with exceptions. The District of Columbia, for example, requires copies of the underlying documents to be furnished at the time of filing. This can include copies of the bad check, a disputed contract, unpaid bills, or traffic reports.

FINDING EVIDENCE, EXPERTS, AND WITNESSES

Be prepared before you file your case by thinking through your complete case and locating any missing evidence. For example, if you had an automobile accident at a particular corner, look for security cameras that may have taken video of the accident. Some stores may recycle tapes only after six or nine months. Try to write down the names of all law enforcement officials present when you had your accident. Ask all witnesses to oral contracts or promises to be available for testimony at trial.

If you need an expert witness, try locating a friend who qualifies and who will not charge too much. Often, cash or items that do not have to be reported on an income tax form will do more to convince an expert witness to appear. If you are in a state where the small claims court maximums are relatively high, the cost of the expert witness may guarantee a win.

Before you hire an expert witness, be sure you know what he or she can bring to the facts of the case that will represent the winning hand. Ask probing questions so that you have an idea of how convincing the witness is going to be under stress. An untested witness may be a hazard on trial day.

If you are subpoenaing law enforcement officials, ask for copies of all their paperwork and any personal contemporaneous records they possess. If you are not furnished copies of any citations, the court clerk should be able to tell you whom to subpoena to obtain the records.

DO YOU NEED AN ATTORNEY'S REVIEW?

Although it is necessary to have an attorney's advice before you even start to put the paperwork together, it is often important to have a second review after you can outline how you expect the case will go at trial. You may find several sources of free or low cost advice in your area. If so, you may want to use one after you know you have a problem or dispute to get advice on your best course of action. Later, when you are filing the papers, get a second review to be sure you have a case you can win.

When you review the case with your legal advisor at this time, you should outline your opening statement and your presentation of any documentary or physical evidence. Also, introduce the witnesses and outline what they can add to your case. Most attorneys will advise you not to have too many witnesses who are just providing the same information. The judge has many cases to complete on the trial day, so he needs just enough information to decide the case and nothing more.

HARD-TO-FIND EVIDENCE OR WITNESSES

If you have tried all the other tricks described in this book to locate the job or residence of the defendant and failed, you may need to hire a detective. The Web services listed in Appendix B are good but not perfect. You can have the court clerk look for other judgments against the defendant to identify an address or a fellow claimant seeking this defendant. Property records can also be researched at the Registry of Deeds office in your county. Statewide records may also be available to help you find nearby addresses to list for possible service.

CREATING AN ORGANIZER FOR THE TRIAL DATE

To take the final steps in your organized attack on the defendant, you should create a centralized storage system for all your information. Creating a trial notebook is a good idea. It can have pages on which to write or print information and hold original documents in envelopes designed to fit the rings of the notebook. You should have three copies of all information to circulate to the defendant and judge. The minimum essential information is as follows:

- **The complaint**: You should compile a section with copies of all the filings you have made with the court. Before the trial date, you should visit the clerk to see if all the proof-of-service forms have been returned in a timely fashion, and remember to get a copy to put in your file. This is your backup for any problems within the clerk's office or the court system.

- **Discovery materials**: Whenever possible, you should have copies of all discovery material. Here again, make copies for the judge and the defendant. If the defendant presents evidence you do not have at trial, put it in this file in case you need it for an appeal. Keep copies of any notes you have made with your witnesses so that you will be able to refresh their recollections, should they fail to testify on point at trial.

- **Legal claim outline**: You should have a reference outline from your trips to the law library, showing the legal sections that you believe the defendant violated and any supporting case law that is similar to your case. You want to make it easy for the judge to look up the legal sections or cases that apply. If you have a summary of the legal section from the state code or a summary of the case in question under this section of the law, type it and have it ready for the judge, should he or she ask for it. Do not force the judge to take a copy of the legal citations.

- **Opening statement outline**: You should have an opening statement that outlines your case, details the evidence to be presented, and summarizes the purpose of the testimony of each witness. You may find that organizing this statement onto 3-by-5-inch cards is the best way for you to speak casually from outline points without sounding like a memorized speech.

- **Direct examination questions**: You should have prepared questions in advance for your witnesses, any neutral witnesses (such as law enforcement officials), and the defendant's witnesses. These questions should quickly present to the judge what information the witness can supply, ask a leading question to elicit the information, and, if possible, make the witnesses' testimonies unimpeachable from the defendant's possible questioning. As you receive word of any witnesses the defense plans to call, contact them, if possible, to find out what their testimony will be. Prepare questions that will counter any damages these witnesses might elicit.

- **Notes for cross-examination**: You may expect certain questions from the defense of both you and his witnesses. Prepare questions that either extract information counter to the claims the defendant or witness is making, or ask questions that point to an ulterior motive behind a person's testimony.

- **Closing argument outline:** Try to anticipate all the favorable and unfavorable information that is going to be presented to the judge and prepare a short closing statement. Any notes you have for this, whether on paper or 3-by-5-inch cards, should have space for additional notes. As the trial progresses, note any issues you might encounter and turn them into points for your side or points the defendant makes that the judge may consider devalued.

- **Other miscellaneous exhibits and documents**: Your trial organizer should have safe storage locations for any documents, pictures, or drawings you plan to present. Make sure they are easy to get out of their storage area, as you may wish to post them on an easel or other exhibition device. A good drawing that shows your point of view — for example, in an automobile accident case — can present evidence your way throughout the trial.

VISITING THE COURT BEFORE YOUR TRIAL

When going to trial, you need to be at ease with the court you will be using for your trial and, if possible, with the judge who will hear your case. Ask the court clerk how the judges are rotated in the small claims court so that you can establish the person who is likely to hear your case, what cases are presented, and how the judge reacts. Although it is unlikely that you can fool a judge into ignoring a bad case by using his favorite types of presentations, the opposite is true. You can mishandle a good case and lose it because you present the facts in an unacceptable fashion. You should visit the court often enough so that you feel confident in your ability to present a good case wen it comes time.

SUMMARY

Now, you should know how to complete steps on your **Small Claims Court Checklist (Figure 1.1)**. You should have filed all your pretrial paperwork and prepared all your necessary statements to the court, questions for the witnesses, and gathered your side's evidence. You should have organized all the material you need to rehearse and present your case and spent time in small claims court watching other cases so that you know what to expect on your trial day.

CHAPTER 8:

POTENTIAL PROBLEMS BEFORE THE COURT DATE

In some cases, after filing the paperwork with the court and paying your court-mandated fees and costs, you have only taken the first step toward getting a meaningful court date. A number of problems can occur after you leave the court clerk's office. The sections of this chapter will focus on what problems may occur and how to deal with them.

WHERE IS THE DEFENDANT?

The first issue in most small claims court cases is the location of the defendant. It is not uncommon to find that the type of individual that finds himself or herself as a target of lawsuits does so many times. Most of such individuals develop a strategy to make locating them for service into court difficult. You must be prepared to use a number of tools to locate the individual for service.

POSTAL OR PRIVATE MAILBOX HOLDER

The first problem may involve witnesses or defendants who receive their mail at a post office box rather than a physical street address. The U.S. Postal Service has a means of supplying a forwarding address but may not release a physical address in all cases. In some states, you may have the court clerk's office assist you in finding the defendant or a witness who has a post office box address. See the following sample form in **Figure 8.1**.

FIGURE 8.1: REQUEST TO POST OFFICE FOR BOXHOLDER'S ADDRESS

Postmaster Assistance

Municipal Court San Bernardino County   JT1430-1281

Name and address of Court: Small Claims Case Number:

44191 Sage Highway, Joshua Tree CA XXXXX

SERVICE OF THE POSTMASTER

REQUEST FOR NEEDED BOXHOLDER INFORMATION

FOR SERVICE OF PERSONAL APPEARANCE DOCUMENTS

OR DELIVERY OF DOCUMENTS AND THINGS AT TRIAL OR HEARING AND

CLARIFICATION

IN THE MATTER OF THE PEOPLE OF THE STATE OF CALIFORNIA, TO:

Mary Ganis, P.O. Box 244, Desert View, CA XXXXX

FOR SERVICE TO APPEAR AS A WITNESS in the case at the date, time, and place shown in the box below UNLESS I DO CERTIFY BELOW THAT THE SERVICE CAN ONLY BE ACCOMPLISHED AS REQUIRED BY LAW FOR COURT ON THE DATE AND TIME BELOW IF PHYSICAL ADDRESS INFORMATION IS SUPPLIED:

Date:	Time:	Dept.:	Div.:	Room:
June 12, 20XX	9 a.m.	189	DV	102

Address:
44191 Sage Highway, Joshua Tree, CA XXXXX

1. The authorized server's address, including phone number, appears on the attached postpaid envelope. Please provide the physical address of the above boxholder to:

Harry Wells, Coster Paralegal, 711 Court House Court, Joshua Tree, CA Phone (XXX) XXX-XXXX

2. Said person serving is qualified under the law as follows:

(1) ☐ A registered California process server.

(2) ☐ A California sheriff, marshal, or constable.

FIGURE 8.1: REQUEST TO POST OFFICE FOR BOXHOLDER'S ADDRESS

(3) ☐Not a registered California Process server.

(4) ☐Employee or independent contractor of a registered California process server.

(5) ☐Exempt from registration under Professions Code 2250(b).

(6) ☐Registered professional photocopier.

(7) ☑Exempt from registration under Professions Code 22451.

I declare under penalty of perjury under the laws of this state that the boxholder address request herein made is a lawful request under the laws of this state and 18 USC section 1001.

Karen Millard

Date Issued: May 23, 20XX Associate Court Clerk Official

FIGURE 8.2: PERSONAL REQUEST FOR DEFENDANT OR WITNESS INFORMATION

John Smith

123 Main Street

Desert View, CA XXXXX

May 23, 20XX

Postmaster

Desert View, CA XXXXX

RE: Request for boxholder information needed for service of legal process under Title 18 USC section 1001

Please furnish the name and street address for the following post office boxholder

Marko Harrison

P.O. Box 1022

FIGURE 8.2: PERSONAL REQUEST FOR DEFENDANT OR WITNESS INFORMATION

Desert View, CA XXXXX

The following is furnished to substantiate the properness and legality of this request:

1. Capacity of requestor (e.g., process server, attorney, party represent self): Party represent self.

2. Statute or regulation that empowers me to serve process (not required when requestor is an attorney or party acting pro se — except a corporation acting pro se must site statute): I am a party representing myself.

3. The name of all known parties to the litigation: John Smith, Plaintiff, and Marko Harrison, Defendant.

4. The court in which the case has been, or will be heard: Municipal Court San Bernardino County, 44191 Sage Highway, Joshua Tree CA XXXXX, Department 189, Division DV, and Room 102.

5 The docket or other identifying number, if one has been issued: Case Number XX-DV-XXXXX.

6. The capacity in which this individual is to be served (e.g., defendant or witness): Defendant.

WARNING: THE SUBMISSION OF FALSE INFORMATION TO OBTAIN AND USE BOXHOLDER INFORMATION FOR ANY PURPOSE OTHER THAN THE SERVICE OF LEGAL PROCESS IN CONJUNCTION WITH ACTUAL OR PROSPECTIVE LITIGATION COULD RESULT IN CRIMINAL PENALTIES INCLUDING A FINE OF UP TO $10,000 OR IMPRISONMENT OF NOT MORE THAN 5 YEARS OR BOTH.

I certify that the above information is true and that the address information is needed and will be used solely for service of legal process in conjunction with actual or prospective litigation.

John Smith

Chicago Public Library
Greater Grand Crossing
3/3/2016   5:56:04 PM
-Patron Receipt-

ITEMS BORROWED:

1:
Title: Making sense of phonics : the hows
Item #: R0430126084
Due Date: 3/24/2016

2:
Title: How to win your case in small claim
Item #: R0430147933
Due Date: 3/24/2016

-Please retain for your records-

In other states, you will need to draft your own request on plain paper or stationery that complies with the U.S. Postal Service's regulations and laws for the release of private information. One of the few purposes in which the U.S. Postal Service will release boxholder information is under Title 18 USC Section 1001 for service of a witness or defendant in a legal action.

With this method of obtaining the address of a witness or defendant, style it after the exhibit in **Figure 8.2: Personal Request for Defendant or Witness Information**. You must supply information in each of the six statements listed on the letter.

If the boxholder is holding a box at a private mailbox service, you may obtain this information through the postmaster for the street address of that service. These boxholders are required to fill out a form with the private mailbox service company listing their physical address and file a copy with the local postmaster. In practice, the information you receive from the postmaster may be fictitious, as it is never checked against other postal records, unless there is a request under Title 18 USC Section 1001 or there is an attempt to forward mail after a private mailbox is closed.

ISSUES RELATED TO SERVICE OF THE DEFENDANT

Service on the defendant and important witnesses must occur in a timely manner before a trial can take place. Bad information about where defendants and witnesses can be found has to be corrected to assure the best chance of service. The method of service is most important after you have an ironclad address where the defendant or witness can be served. There are several ways to go about service. Some depend on your state's law, so verify your choice with the court clerk's office. The common means are as follows:

- **Personal service** : This is the type of service where someone simply hands the document to the defendant and walks away. That person will record the service on a proof-of-service form, as shown in the previous chapter, and return the proof-of-service document to the court. The common methods of personal service are:

1. **Sheriff, marshal, or constable**: All states allow personal service by law officers, although the busier offices are moving away from the business of civil service to concentrate on criminal activity.

2. **Private process servers**: Many states allow private companies or individuals to be private process servers. This is a business that is easy to get into, and, therefore, it attracts fly-by-night operators that may do a poor job. Companies that furnish other legal services often are more professional and will do a better job. Check with your court clerk for recommendations, or look in the phone directory for a firm that has been in the business for a long time.

3. **Service by a disinterested person**: In some states, anyone who is not directly or indirectly tied to the case or its parties may serve as an independent disinterested server. In most cases, the server must be an adult, but the age varies from state to state. Few states consider a relative far enough removed from the case to perform the service.

- **Service by the mails**: Some states allow service of witnesses or defendants by the U.S. Postal Service. Be careful what service you select from the post office, as its services are not always recognized by the court. As indicated elsewhere, service by mail is easy to evade, so your potential witness or difficult defendant may ignore this method.

- **First-class mail**: A few states accept first-class mail as a means of service. The presumption here is that if mailed from the court and not returned as undeliverable, the witness or defendant is considered served. Other states will accept the service as fulfilled if the version of first-class mail, called Priority Mail with Delivery Confirmation is used.

- **Certified mail**: The majority of states accept certified mail as a form of service, but again, it is easy for the defendant to avoid the postal service's notices of an attempt to deliver certified mail.

- **Substitute service or "nail and mail"**: The details of substitute service vary from state to state. In some cases, you need only to affix a copy to the door of a defendant's residence or place of work in a manner where it cannot be removed by natural forces (this is the "nail" part) and on the same day you deposit it in the U.S. mail (this is the "mail" part). Variations include serving another person at the residence or place of work and mailing the service document copy the same day. In most cases, when a substitute person is served, he or she must be informed to whom the document is sent, the general contents of the document, and the date of trial appearance.

WHO SHOULD BE SERVED?

The matter for serving business are different than serving an indivudal. They are as follows:

- **Sole proprietorship**: Serve the owner.

- **Partnership**: Serve at least one of the partners.

- **Limited partnership**: Serve the partner who runs the business. This is normally the person who carries the title of managing partner. If the partnership has registered an agent for service with the state, you should serve this agent (often an attorney).

- **Corporation (profit or nonprofit)**: Serve an officer — president, vice president, secretary, or treasurer.

- **Limited liability company or corporation**: Serve an officer — president, vice president, secretary, or treasurer. In some states, this may include a managing member.

- Government agency: File an administrative claim with the agency first, much like a demand letter, then within the specified time for your state, call the agency and ask who accepts service for the agency.

It is the plaintiff's responsibility to make sure the papers have been served on the defendant and any necessary witnesses before the court date. Know this date, and plan to spend enough effort to assure the papers will be served within this time. Make sure the court will have the proof-of-service documents in its hands according to the court deadlines. If the defendant or adverse or reluctant witnesses have been served late, consider rescheduling the case. If the defendant asks for a postponement, take control of the case from the start and move the court date forward, before the defendant demands it.

DEFENDANT'S RIGHT TO AN ATTORNEY

The defendant has the right to be represented by an attorney. If he files to be represented by an attorney, there will likely be a request for a postponement. Do not fight it. You may not win the point with the court and possibly prejudice your case on the actual court date. Do not appear irrational or prone to ill-mannered behavior, as this conduct will be remembered by the judge on the trial date. You should have a strategy to deal with this from the beginning, and you may want to have a trained advocate on your side as well.

If the case does not involve much money and your legal advisors and legal research tell you that you have a strong and compelling case, go ahead with your plans to act as your own attorney. If you are at the maximum for small claims court and are not expecting to be fully compensated even if you win, consider moving to a higher court with an attorney.

DEFENDANT STRATEGIES TO AVOID GOING TO TRIAL

Some defendants will attempt to throw up roadblocks to going to trial. It is quite easy to complicate a case with countersuits and counterclaims. You will have to analyze and deal with these as they appear. If you have an idea of what countersuits or counterclaims are possible, try to build your case from the beginning to neutralize these potential hazards. If the defendant claims facts for which you had not prepared a defense, immediately think of a counter-strategy. If necessary, postpone the case to add a witness that can eliminate the countersuit or counterclaim.

The issues you must win are those where the defendant may use a countering strategy. The issues of venue and statute of limitations are easy to attack and defend if you know your legal points. Be prepared for one or both of these to come up before you can even start an opening argument. The defendant may make motions that have to be heard ahead of the actual trial. If it is a contract case and calls for arbitration or mediation, you can be sure to the defense will invoke this contract clause requirement.

FIGURE 8.3: SAMPLE COUNTERSUIT COMPLAINT

Keenan Williams
114 Shady Lane
Rural Route 6
Coster, TN XXXXX
555-515-5900

Plaintiff Pro Per

The Superior Court of Pioneer Town
County of Hasterton

State of Tennessee

Keenan Williams

          Plaintiff

    v.   Case Number _____

Carson Myer   COMPLAINT

FIGURE 8.3: SAMPLE COUNTERSUIT COMPLAINT

Defendant   JURY TRIAL DEMANDED

1. On approximately April 19, 20XX, at 3:30 p.m., ESD, while Plaintiff was driving his automobile with his aged mother on board to a needed doctor's appointment in Coster on Highway 232, in Hasterton County, Defendant Carson Myer did negligently weave from the bike path into the path of Plaintiff Keenan Williams' automobile.

2. As a result of the Defendant's negligent bicycle riding, the Plaintiff's aged mother suffered a heart attack, causing substantial pain and suffering and medical expense.

WHEREFORE, Plaintiff prays for judgment against the defendant of $15,000 plus costs and interest.

Keenan Williams
_____

Keenan Williams, Plaintiff in Pro Per
Plaintiff demands trial by jury

Be sure you have shared all your evidence with the defendant. If he or she fails to provide evidence to you that he or she knows exists and is prepared to present, object to its introduction because of failure to share it in discovery. If all evidence has been shared to support a countersuit or counterclaim, be prepared to defend yourself just as firmly as you will present the central points of your dispute with the defendant.

In **Figure 8.3: Sample Countersuit Complaint**, we see the defendant of an earlier case presented in Chapter 3 telling his side of the case by filing a claim against the plaintiff of the original suit. Although the complaint is short, you can see that each party has a different view of what happened on the day in question. The introduction of the aged mother into the case suggests a hint of a new witness the original plaintiff may not have expected. Due to possible bias, this witness could shed light on a different legal cause of the accident.

STATE-REQUIRED ALTERNATIVES TO TRIAL

If your case is one that requires mediation before the court can hear the case, use the mechanism to win your case's maximum. If the defendant acts in a conciliatory manner and is willing to make immediate payment, you might consider settling for less than your original amount. Make fulfillment of this payment a condition of the settlement. In some states, it is possible a promise in the reconciliation session will not be kept, and the mediation allows both parties to reach a settlement and have the court issue a judgment necessary to enforce the agreement. You do not want to return to court to fight over a settlement that was never fulfilled.

SUMMARY

This chapter has dealt with issues and problems that may occur after the case is filed but before the trial date is set. This chapter explained the defendant's rights and the extensive arsenal of tools he or she has to fight the case. Many defendants think a dispute will never go to court. In this chapter, you find that this is not always realistic. Like a trout on the end of your fishing line, you will find there are many skillful maneuvers you can make to net the fish and win your judgment.

CHAPTER 9:

PREPARING FOR YOUR DAY IN COURT

After you have filed the necessary papers with the court to start your case, you must get organized for the work you will need to do in court before the judge or jury. Depending on your vision of the opponent and expectations from the witnesses or experts, you must have your questions ready for every contingency.

You will need an opening statement, a list of the legal issues in your particular case, and the presentation of the case details that will convince the court or jury of your position. In some cases, you may have documentary evidence to present and explain to the judge. Where there are witnesses, you will need to pose questions to elicit your points on the issues. If you have hired an expert, organize with him or her which testimony ought to be presented to have a positive impact on your case. If the opponent appears to have a well-organized case, you should devise a strategy to discount this material, and, if possible, make the evidence support your case.

FORMAL DISCOVERY

When preparing your case, you will be engaged in what the court calls discovery. This is evidence-gathering, including locating witnesses, compelling testimony, and obtaining documentary proof—audio material, electronic tapes, videos, and printed matter that show evidence in the case. Under the Federal Rule of Civil Procedure (FRCP) Rule 26(b), you and your adversary may request any information made in the pleadings. This includes identifying witnesses who have facts and interviewing them to see if they possess unique information that supports your case, which covers information from electronic sources, such as e-mail messages and computer files, even if they have never taken printed form.

Your job at discovery is to obtain information favorable to your story to be presented to the judge or jury. You may use information found in discovery to locate evidence your adversary is likely to use against you. Finally, you can use discovery interviews to lock in testimony for later use in trial. All meetings with perspective witnesses should be recorded and/or transcribed to use to discredit the witness should one later change the story.

Most states have streamlined discovery rules and laws, fashioned after the federal rules, which require the voluntarily disclosure of information to the opponent. Included in the mandatory sharing of information with your opponent are the identities of your expert witnesses and their qualifications. Also, present a list of other witnesses you plan to call, the relevance of any documents you plan to use as exhibits, the existence of tangible objects you plan to produce for display to the court, and any insurance agreements that relate to the case.

Formal discovery means you cannot blindside an opponent with a piece of evidence you have hidden from his view or discovered by means that the opponent may not had available in his gathering of evidence. If you are in doubt, disclose the information to your opponent.

The form used for the disclosure varies from state to state. Some require you to provide a copy if the evidence itself makes this suitable. In other cases, you need only to notify the opponent that you have made a discovery of a certain type while investigating a particular document, witness, or scene of the event. If your state requires this type of limited discovery notification, you may need to supply names of witnesses and their phone numbers. Also, provide enough reference details of other information for the opponent to evaluate it without a major search of relevant records.

In most cases, you must provide this discovery information to your opponent at least a month before the trial date. Some states require a process of asking questions from defendant to plaintiff and plaintiff to defendant during the month preceding the court date. In a few cases, the interchanges are totally unlimited, so it is best not to hide information you will later be forced to disclose.

SELECTING THE JURY

The process of selecting a jury is called by the French term, *voir dire*, which means to select a jury by asking questions that give the judge and parties information about the juror's feelings, experiences, and knowledge. Juries are normally called to serve in a jury pool over time, perhaps two weeks or a month. Its members are later selected from the pool to serve on a particular jury. In small claims court cases, the jury size may be from six to 12. You can use a jury selecting tool such as the card shown on **Figure 9.1: Sample Jury Selection Aid**. It should have space for the number of jurors that will serve in your case (check with the court clerk to find out how many are normal).

The jurors will be selected at random and brought to the juror's box as a group. Normally, the judge asks the jurors questions about their occupations and background. When the judge is finished asking questions, each plaintiff or defendant may question individual jurors whom are identified only by number. If there are multiple plaintiffs or defendants, they may each have a turn at asking questions.

As the judge and other parties ask questions, you should make notes on the selection aid card on issues you feel might make the juror biased against your cause or case. Later, you will be allowed to challenge certain jurors. But before doing this, you should ask the clerk's office how many challenges you will be allowed to make without giving a reason and the number you can make with a stated justification. This varies from state to state.

FIGURE 9.1: SAMPLE JURY SELECTION AID		
Jury 1		
Juror 1	Juror 2	Juror 3
Juror 4	Juror 5	Juror 6
Juror 7	Juror 8	Juror 9
Juror 10	Juror 11	Juror 12
Alternate 1		
Alternate 2		
Alternate 3		

After all questions have been answered, it is time for juror challenges. The type where you do not have to state your reason for your challenge is called the peremptory challenge. Each plaintiff, or defendant, may ask the judge if a particular juror can be excused. It is the judge's decision to make, but normally he or she follows the desires of the parties on this type of challenge.

There are also challenges for cause available to each party. In this latter case, you must say your reason for the challenge to the judge, and he must rule that the bias you claim is persuasive. If you feel the reason you are going to give for dismissing the juror may be inflammatory, you are allowed to make a challenge for cause in chambers. It is better to do this than to irritate the remaining jurors who are listening to challenges for cause.

In some states, alternates are also chosen for small claims courts. If this is the case, part of the selected jury will be designated as jury members and as alternates, to serve in numerical order. It is important to note that each party has challenges that do not have to be supported by a reason. The jury selection process can continue for a long time if both parties overuse the process.

If the jury size drops below the minimum for the trial, new jurors will be brought from the jury pool, and the questioning cycle starts again. Some states start with an extended jury, then randomly select the number needed when the challenge process has finished. You should always ask the court clerk the rules of that particular courtroom.

THE OPENING STATEMENT

You will need to have an opening statement to the judge or jury that briefly outlines your case and what you plan to present in support of your position. As described previously, you should carry a case notebook with your evidence and presentation materials inside. One of the major elements of the notebook should be some note cards with the outline of your case.

Figure 9.2: Sample Opening Statement Card outlines the kind of material you may wish to put on the card for your opening statement. Although all cases are different, this example shows some points that all opening statements should include. First, you should place a large number, possibly in the upper right-hand corner, on each card. If you get nervous and drop your cards in court or the case does not go as you planned, you can reorganize the cards to meet your needs while standing before the court.

The opening statement should be addressed to the judge, even if it is a jury trial. Normally, the service of judges in particular courts is scheduled well in advance, so you should be able to ask the court clerk who will hear your case. Make your opening brief yet as concise as possible, without testifying for yourself. To simplify the procedures, one case has been selected for the preparation of a set of case cards along with the day in court materials. The case selected is presented in the complaint (**Figure 3.2: Sample Typed Civil Complaint**), and the countersuit (**Figure 8.3: Sample Countersuit Complaint**).

FIGURE 9.2: SAMPLE OPENING STATEMENT CARD
Opening 2

Judge Martin:

My name is Carson Myer. I am a welder at the local James Auto Exhaust Company in the Hasterton Industrial Park. I am an avid bicycle rider and supporter of traffic-sheltered bike trails, such as the one we have in the county along the Scenic Old West Highway.

It was there that I was recently injured by an automobile that failed to yield the right-of-way to my bike and myself in the bike path. As you can see from the easel presentation on my left, the state has adopted uniform signs and laws for these sheltered bike areas.

I have suffered more than the state's legal limit on small claims cases due to the defendant's failure to yield to me in the bike path, which sent me to the hospital with both a broken leg and arm. Here are some copies of the pictures that the police took at the scene of the accident.

FIGURE 9.3: SAMPLE NOTES OF LEGAL ISSUES CARD
The Law 3

Judge Smith:

As I have been able to do research at the junior college law library, I find that the pertinent legal references for this automobile and bicycle case is Section 141 of the state's annotated statutes. The law protects bike riders from an automobile's

---

FIGURE 9.3: SAMPLE NOTES OF LEGAL ISSUES CARD

encroachment on their driving space, even if there is no protected bike path. When there are designated bike paths, the state's maximum speed laws are all set to a level of 10 miles per hour below the normal stated mandated limits. The law also states that in the case of an accident between an automobile and a bike, the presumed responsible party is the automobile driver unless there are at least two witnesses willing to testify that the bicycle rider was clearly at fault.

Fault is also presumed to be that of the law enforcement officer who took the accident report and issued citations for violations of traffic laws, if any. In this case, Mr. Williams was cited for failure to yield to a bike in a bike path and for failure to carry the state's mandated minimum liability insurance.

For any small claims court case, be ready to present the legal justifications for your position. In most cases, this will simply be a summary and citation of a particular section of the state laws relative to your case. **Figure 9.3: Sample Notes of Legal Issues Card** shows the legal theories at issue in our bike path case. The defendant should have a different legal justification for his actions or case law that cites exceptions relevant to the case in progress.

Your case notebook should have copies of all evidence that you plan to produce, as well as the information the defense has indicated to you that it plans to use. This should include — but not be limited to — any documentary evidence such as contracts, police reports, police citations, or canceled checks that prove payments. If you have photographs illustrating the issues of the case, make sure you have copies in the notebook. If you are using an expert witness, you should have written documentation showing the expert's capabilities or qualifications.

Interview any relevant witnesses and decipher what they might add to the trial. Do not present two witnesses who only testify to the same thing. If, however, one witness saw only part of the incident and another saw a different partial view, use both. Limit their questions to specifics that they can verify. Having a witness say that they "really do not know" something makes their value for your purpos in court immune. Delete that person from your list right away.

If you have made attempts to settle the matter in the past, any documentary evidence is beneficial. If you issued a demand letter before going to trial, present it as proof that you need the court's assistance in resolving the matter. If there has been any formal or informal arbitration, present all written evidence of it or summarize the positions of both sides to the judge.

Obtain a pair of blank judgment forms, available at the court clerk's office, and prepare them for the judge. Furnish one with the exact settlement amount you are requesting in the complaint. Fill out the second form with all information on the form, except the settlement amount. At the end of the trial, the judge may ask if you have prepared a judgment. Make both forms available, and let the judge write down his decision. The judge will hand it to the clerk for filing after court is over.

WITNESS TESTIMONY

You should interview your and your opponent's witnesses. Take notes and integrate them into witness question cards for your court day presentation. **Figure 9.4: Sample Questioning of Witness Card** and **Figure 9.5: Sample Cross-Examination Questions Card** show typical notes for questioning of witnesses. Remember, the questions should be designed to bring out your side of the argument and keep either opponent information or extraneous information out of the discourse. You will occasionally find witnesses who like to extend their answers, so be prepared with the next question to prevent long extemporaneous answers.

When you question the witnesses for the other side, you should be careful not to expose what other witnesses may present. If there is a contradiction, you want to be the only person to know it. If you are aware of conflicting information in advance, you may be able to plan your questions to the opposing witnesses in such a way as to elicit testimony different from what they gave in the pretrial questioning. In our examples, study the questions and expected answers of the two witnesses to the accident.

When you have an idea of what the witnesses will say, you have a chance to gather any additional and worthwhile evidence. In our bike path case, the automobile driver claims there were no bike path markings. In this case, a few pictures will easily defeat this statement. If the skid marks, which the police report mentioned, are still visible, then add these to your picture exhibit portfolio.

If your case uses police or other sworn service personnel, it is wise to interview them first. Give the official an opportunity to review the case a second time before the trial. Try to ascertain what, if any, holes the officer will leave in the case. Knowing this key testimony in advance will allow you to contact witnesses or arrange experts to complete your case and make it convincing.

FIGURE 9.4: SAMPLE QUESTIONING OF WITNESS CARD

Witness Jelus 5

Q: It is my understanding that you witnessed the accident from a good position across the highway. Is that correct? (Expected: Yes.)

Q: Can you explain what you saw? (Expected: The driver of the car was not paying attention because he was on his cellular phone.)

Q: Did you notice the driver speaking in an animated fashion on his cellular phone? (Expected: Yes; He appeared to be quite angry at someone.)

Q: Did it appear to you that the driver was in the bike lane? (Expected: Yes; I am sure of it!)

Q: Did the driver brake before hitting me? (Expected: There were no brake lights.)

Q: I understand you told the police that you thought the auto driver was erratic? (Expected: Yes, I did. He definitely was.)

You may find you need time to subpoena information from your opponent or others whom are either involved or can substantiate details of the dispute. Gather the information by using your subpoena power through the small claims court clerk's office. Collect public records, such as traffic surveillance tapes and property records. Also, search for other court cases involving the opponent, then put the information in your notebook.

As you develop the outline of how you think the trial day will go, make cards for your presentation. Make copies of documents you can leave with the judge and the opponent. In most states, there are rights of discovery that compel both parties to share information about the case with each other. Take advantage of the information you get from your opponent to surmise what he might propose in court.

If possible, have a graphic that you can display on an easel or pass out to focus your presentation of the real issues of the case. If it is a matter of one person's words versus another, try to show the illogical flaw of the excuse that your opponent is using. If there are facts that can be graphically presented, get a drawing, map, photograph, or different display of the object.

FIGURE 9.5: SAMPLE ANALYSIS OF EVIDENCE CARD
Easel Photo 48
The photographic enlargement that I have placed on the easel was taken of a sign which Keenan Williams passed on Scenic Old West Highway approximately three-fifths of a mile before he hit me while I was in the bicycle path.
You will notice that the sign carries both the official international bike path marker and the state-supplied yield for bicycles signs. The defendant, in his opening statement, stated flatly that there were no markings on the highway directing him to yield the right of way to my bike.
I measured the distance between these signs on the Scenic Old West Highway for at least 20 miles before my accident site. The state has put these signs approximately every two miles throughout the entire distance.

CROSS-EXAMINATION

As your opposition puts on its case, you should carefully take notes of any unexpected evidence or testimony. If you have a witness or evidence card for the presentation, make these notes on the back of the card and circle the number on the front of the card to remind you that there are new questions to be asked. You do not want to leave any accusations from your opponent unchallenged, as this can hurt your case. It is best to ask leading questions up to the critical issue, then spring questions that challenge the statements or credibility of the witness.

As you begin the cross-examination of the opposition's witnesses, attempt to start in a calm and matter-of-fact manner. Try to develop an indirect path of questions that will lead to the issue you want devalued. In our example cross-examination, **Figure 9.6: Sample Cross-examination Questions Card**, the witness said that the defendant was on his cellular phone and appeared not to be paying attention to his driving.

The cross-examination witness had a different view (see **Figure 11.3: Sample Auto Accident Report**) from the rear of your opponent's car. Due to the dark tinted windows, he may not have observed the cellular phone in use. Be skillful, and bring out facts by approaching them through another issue. In this case, it is the existence of his mother as a passenger in the back seat of the car. Either her presence or the dark tint of the windows denied the witness the chance to see the person talking on his cellular phone.

FIGURE 9.6: SAMPLE CROSS-EXAMINATION QUESTIONS CARD

Cross Gerstat 11

Expected Testimony: The witness claims to have been behind the auto driver, and did not see any indication of cellular phone use.

Q: Mr. Gerstat, I understand you testified that you did not see any cellular phone being used. Is that correct? (Expected: Yes.)

Q: Did you know there was a passenger in the rear seat of the Explorer? (Expected: No.)

Q: Did you know that the Explorer, which Mr. Williams was driving, had an extra dark rear window? (Expected: No.)

FIGURE 9.6: SAMPLE CROSS-EXAMINATION QUESTIONS CARD

Q: Was it the Explorer's dark-tinted windows that prevented you from seeing Mr. Williams' aged mother in the back seat of the car? (Expected: Yes, I suppose.)

Q: Assuming you could not see the passenger, how could you be sure that Mr. Williams was not talking on his cellular phone? (Expected: I guess I cannot be sure about that.)

It is possible to encounter cross-examination witnesses that are related or biased toward your opposition. You may be able to suggest that the judge declare the witness a hostile witness so you can limit answers to yes or no. This makes questioning easier, as you can say the information that you need to have heard in court. If you do your homework on whom the opponent plans to use as a witness, you should be able to discover any relationships you can point out in your questioning that will invalidate the testimony of the witness.

PRESENTING EVIDENCE

As you develop your case notebook, try to gather as much evidence as you possibly can. You want to be prepared for any contingency your opponent may bring forth as an excuse to accept his or her side of the argument. If the matter is covered by such written or printed items as contracts, canceled checks, or receipts, have them compiled in your notebook. All documents should be clearly labeled as not to hide the details on them and numbered to correspond with your cue cards.

If your case is one that lends itself well to photographic evidence, go out and take the pictures. Organize both the wide and closely detailed pictures and have them printed in at least 5-by-7-inch format, (8.5-by-11-inch paper is better). Typed or printed labels that clearly identify the picture should be placed uniformly on the picture. Number these for reference in your presentation cards.

FIGURE 9.7: SAMPLE CLOSING ARGUMENT CARD

Closing 20

Judge Martin:

My evidence and witnesses have presented a clear picture that the defendant carelessly hit me in the bike path, causing great bodily harm and inordinate financial loss.

The defendant has tried to prove that I was weaving outside the bicycle path but has been unable to do so. I had witness testimony pointing to his careless cellular phone use. I have impeached his witness, who finally accepted the likelihood that he would not have been able to see if he were using his cellular phone.

I pray that you will carefully examine the pictures, police reports, and witness evidence to rule in favor of the plaintiff in the amount of $15,000.

THE CLOSING ARGUMENT

As with your opening statement, your closing argument should be made directly to the judge. It should consist of a short summary of your case and a statement discounting your opponent's case. A cue card for the closing argument is shown in **Figure 9.7: Sample Closing Argument Card.**

It is important that you express your statement in a positive fashion. There should be no negative comments toward your opponent or anger in your voice. You want your case position to be the reasonable choice for the judicial decision. Try cautiously to impress on the judge that you were wronged but that you seek only retribution and not revenge. Always close by asking for a judgment in the amount that you originally requested.

If the clerk has told you in advance that the judge may want you to prepare a judgment statement for his or her signature, you may indicate that you have both a completed and a blank judgment statement form ready. Permit the judge to ask you for the forms before you place them on his desk or table.

In some states, the plaintiff of the case (or the first party filing a case where the trial is a consolidation of cases or includes one or more countersuits or counterclaims), may be allowed both a closing argument and a rebuttal closing. This occurs after the opponent has made a closing statement. When this happens, you should focus your rebuttal to just the points of the opponent's closing. Do not rehash issues you covered in your initial closing.

SUMMARY

The primary purpose of this chapter was to assist you in getting your case organized for trial. The documents gathered or prepared here should allow you to rehearse your presentation and examination of the witnesses and evidence that make up the case. You should try to visualize your case through the opposition's eyes and prepare your attack on the likely positions of your opponent. Using this knowledge, you ought to visit the court where you will be presenting your case. Evaluate your planned strategy against those that the judge, who will be hearing your case, accepts.

If you are the defendant in a small claims court action, you should also be preparing your case along the lines shown in this chapter. Try to build a case that your opponent cannot destroy in cross-examination. Prepare your witnesses for the expected assault that the trial may bring, and carefully select a strategy that rationally shows that you are either the wronged party or not at fault for the deeds that the other side has claimed.

CHAPTER 10:

THE NEED, SELECTION, AND USE OF AN EXPERT WITNESS

Trials, even those in small claims court, can hinge on issues that require an expert to give testimony. You may find a local government official or state employee who can act as an expert, and you wold not have to pay more than travel expenses. In our bike path case example, the safety of highway markings for bike paths can become an issue. In this case, the driver was talking on a cellular phone while driving, and certainly, this could have safety issues.

DO YOU NEED AN EXPERT WITNESS?

You may be able to get a traffic engineer from a nearby city to testify on the effectiveness of paint striping lanes and sign placement. If the person is local, he or she may have specific statistics for the site of the accident. If you cannot find a local traffic engineer, try contacting the state transportation or highway department for data: Perhaps someone can interpret it for you in court. This public exposure may offer him or her a good opportunity to promote traffic safety.

In other types of cases, it might be equally important to find an expert to testify on a key issue on which the case may hinge. For example, if you are an electrical contractor and cannot get paid by the general contractor, the building or electrical inspector responsible for the quality control on the project under the building code may be a good person to have testify. If you say you did the work and the inspector agrees that it was completed up to code, you deserve to be paid.

Expert witnesses do not have to be hired guns or professionals who make a living solely by testifying in court. If you have a case where a dairy farm's lease payments are in arrears, a longtime farmer may be an excellent choice to testify about the business aspects of running a dairy. The farmer is not likely to be viewed as a professional just brought to court to win your case and may even testify for nothing more than a handshake.

Your need for an expert is determined by the technical difficulty of the issues at stake and the lack of knowledge about these principals with the court and the public. In our bike path case, most people know about the existence of bike paths and how they are marked along the right-hand side of the road's right lane. If the case required knowledge of normal road crown curvatures for drainage and their effects on the size or safety of bike paths, an expert might be needed. Because this case hinges on the testimony of two witnesses and the police report, an expert witness about bike path design would not deal with the real issues of the case.

CAN YOU AFFORD AN EXPERT WITNESS?

Unless your case is a large one, you may find it difficult to get an expert that you can afford. Expert witnesses normally charge several hundred dollars per hour. The charges may include any necessary research time, travel time, and the entire day of the court trial. You should be careful when investing this kind of money if the case is under $10,000 and filed in small claims court, as you will most likely not be able to include the expert's costs as part of the amount you will be reimbursed — assuming you win the case. If you file the same case pro se in civil court, the practices are different. Here, the winner is often rewarded by having the loser pay the costs, including those of an expert witness.

Some expert testimony can be solidified through a written statement or deposition. If you supply the opposition with a copy of your written information through the discovery rules mentioned in Chapter 9, it is unlikely you will need to pay for the expert to travel and testify on your trial date. If you are claiming that you could not go to work and lost wages or income as a result of the other side's actions, a simple letter from your doctor may be sufficient. Your opponent can always interview the doctor or subpoena him or her to testify if he or she thinks the contention attested to in the letter is incorrect.

One way to find an affordable local witness is to use Craigslist to advertise for someone who can fill your technical needs without burning a hole in your budget. Craigslist has advertising sites on the Internet for every state — most large cities. You can outline your problem, and your opponent will be totally unaware that you are looking for an expert witness, because the service hides your name and e-mail address if you desire.

To use Craigslist to find an expert witness, go to the Web site (**www. Craigslist.org**) and register. It is free and requires only your e-mail address and a password. First, select the city nearest you or your statewide ad site. You will see the menu page shown as **Figure 10.1: Using Craigslist to Locate Inexpensive Local Expert**. Select "event," followed by event gigs, and the area of the city nearest you.

Fill in your ad, as shown in the example **Figure 10.2: Entering My Craigslist Ad for Posting**. First, attempt running the ad without pay, then with pay by asking respondents to bid a price for the work. Try posting by marking the "no pay" box if you have time, as the ad will have to be reposted every seven days. You can check the "pay" box later if you are not getting a response.

The example we have selected is for our bike path case, but you can construct an ad for a suitable expert for almost any type of small claims court case. As shown, the ad includes a phone number, but you do not have to include any personal information. Anyone who answers your ad for an expert witness will have his or her e-mail forwarded to your real e-mail address.

Craigslist has a reputation as being an easy site to read and follow. You will be surprised at the number of answers a single, seven-day ad will generate; plus the service is free on both sides.

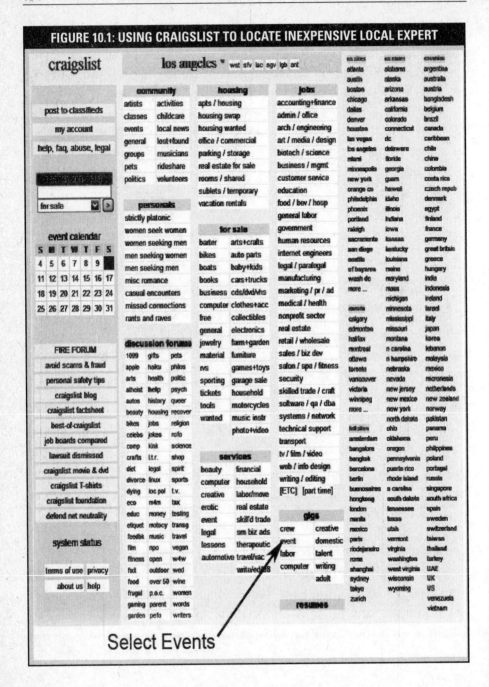

FIGURE 10.1: USING CRAIGSLIST TO LOCATE INEXPENSIVE LOCAL EXPERT

Select Events

FIGURE 10.2: ENTERING MY CRAIGSLIST AD FOR POSTING

Project Title	Specific Location
Seeking Expert on Bike Path Safety	Greater Chattanooga Area

Posting Description:

Looking for bike path expert familiar with safety and accident rates in local bike paths. A major issue may be cellular phone use by drivers traveling near bike paths. Seeking expert for testimony in local small claims court. I am willing to provide donation out of the settlement to the local bike charity of your choice. The trial is about six weeks away, therefore I need to establish immediate contact, so we can work out trial strategy. The case involves an accident where I was riding my bicycle on Scenic Highway and was hit by a driver in the protected and signed bike lane. Please answer ad or call XXX-XXX-XXXX.

__ No Pay __ Pay

Your E-mail Address:

youremailaddress@mail.com

Use this address as my reply-to address.

Reply to gigs-xxxxxxxxx@craigslist.org (Craigslist makes your address anonymous and relays it to you).

Do not show any e-mail address (be sure to put a phone number or other contact information in your posting).

__ OK for others to contact you about other services, products, or commercial interests?

Although our sample ad includes a phone number, it is not advised to use this method unless you have a phone number with either voice mail or an answering machine. Call screening is recommended.

USING THE INTERNET TO LOCATE AND OBTAIN WRITTEN EXPERT OPINIONS

There are several Internet services that will help you locate the right expert witness for your particular case. Try **www.ExpertResources.com** as a source for finding experts on more than 1,200 subjects. You can browse the list and request the credentials of a specific expert or fill out an inquiry form and let the Web firm's search professionals locate several experts that meet your criteria.

The Web site **www.National-Experts.com** specializes in forensic experts. Although these experts can be used in civil cases, they may be more suitable for criminal cases. If you have an issue, such as the tire tracks in our bike path case, you may be able to confirm the testimony of your single witness. The expert may be able to match the tire tracks to the opponent's Ford Explorer and tell the judge that the brakes were applied only after the bicycle was hit.

The Legal Expert Network, **www.expertnetwork.com**, does offer an impressive list of legal experts. Similar to the **www.ExpertResources. com**, it will question you on the phone and develop a group of expert portfolios for you to read before you select an expert witness through the organization.

COURT-APPOINTED EXPERT WITNESSES

If you cannot afford an expert witness, there is a small chance the court will appoint one for you. The principle here is that judges do not consider themselves experts at anything other than the law. Using expert witnesses is a means to inform the judge of the technical details that may decide the case. Federal court procedures mandate that state and local courts have funds allocated in their budgets for experts to aid the court. Most of these allocated funds are spent on criminal cases, but these are legally available to the civil court system, including the small claims court.

The expert witness fund for these witnesses is administered by a single judge in a judicial district. The court clerk can often explain this function and outline the procedure by which you may apply for court assistance in paying for an expert witness. Be sure that the clerk of the small claims court checks with the judge who will hear your case before you make a motion to another judge for an expert witness.

ALTERNATIVES TO AN EXPERT WITNESS

The purpose of the expert witness is to add specialized knowledge to the case that tends to support your side of the case. There may be other ways to do this. For example, the careful use of exhibits from books may point out the correctness of your position. You may find that your local high school or junior college teacher can provide you with exhibits from an appropriate textbook or teacher's manual that will allow you to illustrate your side of the case. In our bike path case, drawings of the state or National Transportation Safety Board standards for bike path sizing and striping may offer expertise as a page enlarged for the easel.

TESTIMONY BY LETTER OR OTHER MEANS

In most small claims courts there are no fixed rules that require an in-person expert testimony in court. You should check with any problems that the judge might have about using an expert witness by letter or video. This may be allowed, and if the opposition is offered a chance to pose questions to the expert in rebuttal, you may eliminate the need for an expert witness appearing. In our bike path case, you could send the expert detailed photographs of the tire tracks, along with court-ordered impressions of the opponent's tires, both of which a local expert could prepare and send to any distant expert witness.

If you use testimony by letter or video, you will need paper documentation to present to the court to allow your information to be brought into the case as evidence. The minimum information would include the name of the witness and a list of credentials that give him or her status for the court as an expert witness as well as work and educational experience.

Although this seems like a large volume, most professional expert witnesses consider these facts crucial in the selection process. The expert will need to be able to render an opinion that is helpful to the issues of the case. In our bike path case, the tire witness needs to be able to identify the tire prints as matching the molds taken of the tires and say that the pattern shows that pressure was not supplied to the brake for about 15 feet, but only after the impact with the bicycle.

The expert will need to discuss how and when he or she analyzed and explained how the chain of custody of the evidence was maintained during the analysis. A brake expert might also be able to give opinions on when the driver reacted to the bicycle on the road. Did it happen before, during, or after he hit the rider? **Figure 10.3: Expert Witness Testimony by Letter** shows an example of how an expert can testify without traveling to court, therefore saving you thousands of dollars in expert witness costs.

The testimony supplied in the letter could have been done through a video conference where the parties had their questions answered, along with the experts giving them his or her opinions. A surprising number of small claims judges will also accept testimony from an expert witness by telephone, if this is arranged in advance through the court clerk's office. If you find that your opponent objects to the introduction of written testimony, such as that in our example, a phone call could allow cross-examination.

FIGURE 10.3: EXPERT WITNESS TESTIMONY BY LETTER
The James Jester Company Serving the Forensic Community for 30 Years 1402 Breckenridge Highway Kenton, KY XXXXX July 20, 20XX

FIGURE 10.3: EXPERT WITNESS TESTIMONY BY LETTER

Case: Carson Myer v. Keenan Williams (Case # 1221-9871-0)

Your Honor:

I am a licensed forensic contractor with more than 30 years of experience, as outlined in my qualifications package attached to this letter. I have been in contact with both parties to this suit to explain my findings and answer any questions they have on those findings. Below are the investigations, which I have completed, and the conclusions I have drawn.

First, I would like to thank your Tennessee Bureau of Investigation (TBI) for executing your subpoena for tire impressions and providing them to me at the fees that are normally used only for the local governments they serve. The evidence was sealed and delivered to my office by common carrier. At that time, I broke the seal and made the analysis. I have resealed the evidence, and it is available for use by any other party in the case.

I have used the normal data for the year of the Explorer involved in the accident with the reported accessories and passengers. I have measurement information from the paint marks the police used to mark the resting point of the bicycle and detailed photographs of all tire tracks or skid marks in the approximately 50 yards on either side of this resting point. As I have indicated to both sides, I believe I have sufficient information to supply a conclusive opinion as to what braking activity occurred, if any, within the period immediately before and after the impact.

It is my considered conclusion that the driver of the Explorer was at fault and had one pair of wheels within the bike path at the time of the accident. Within normal reaction times after impact, the brakes were applied with such force as to bring the vehicle to a full stop in the bike path approximately 55 feet from the impact. Furthermore, there is no data that would indicate that the automobile driver applied the brakes with any significant force to avoid the impact at anytime during the accident.

The tire tracks on the pavement, and the tire impressions of the subpoenaed Explorer, make this the vehicle that hit the bicycle without any reasonable possibility of error.

Sincerely,

James Jester

For the James Jester Company

CHOOSING THE RIGHT EXPERT

The person that you want on your side as an expert witness needs to have the qualifications to convince the court that your claims are valid and reasonable. When looking for an expert, you need to take some careful steps. Often, you may not have to spend money to find the expert. Their marketing costs are not your responsibility. You should first request a résumé or curriculum vitae (CV).

The potential expert witness will likely have a complete background package that he or she is ready to supply you. This is the normal way of selling services, so it should be complete, well organized, and eloquently written. If you are not impressed with the presentation, the judge or jury may not be either. If you contact more than one potential expert witness, examine their credentials carefully before you begin your decision making process. Try to put yourself in the judge's mind set and see which expert is most likely to impress him or her. Your visits to the courtroom prior to your trial date will be valuable here, as you will begin to know the judge's preferences.

Ask for a list of cases for which each expert has been hired recently, and inquire about the side of the argument on which the expert testified. Some witnesses who make good defense expert witnesses could turn out to be poor plaintiff witnesses. Try to analyze any bias that each might have for any particular point of view that is important in your case. Make sure you ask for the reference who hired the expert on each job, and follow up by calling each to ask how effective the witness was to a case. Verify if the witness was the deciding force that brought about a win for the client.

You may find that experts have more skills than you need or that it is hard to see if they have the skills for which you are looking. Call and ask specific questions. Remember, they may be busy traveling and will have to call you back, so write down your questions and be prepared to ask the right questions when they return your call. If you are involved in a malpractice case against a professional such as a doctor, dentist, orthodontist, or lawyer, make sure they know what constitutes malpractice for this profession in your state.

Before you sign any contract to hire an expert, analyze your legal position in the case. Is the testimony critical, does it simply add evidence, or does it merely bring a professional skill to the trial that might otherwise be lacking? Will the expert witness set a tone or level of discourse that raises the case? Most of all, if you are not honest with your expert, you should not expect too much of that expert in performing his or her job properly.

If you have sufficient time before the trial, talk to more than one expert about the case. You may find there are questions that need to be answered for your case that you had not considered. You may also learn that your potential expert witness would be unwilling to render a favorable decision to the question that you want the expert to answer.

Do not be satisfied with the first potential expert witness who can issue an opinion that favors your case. Questioning of additional witnesses may tell you that other witnesses have a larger base of knowledge and can verify your needed opinion from a number of disciplines. Prepare to challenge your potential expert witness with many questions. You should not be intimidated into accepting what looks good on paper. If the person is good, he or she will have undergone difficult questioning in the past.

Find out if each potential expert has represented both points of view in other cases. If one has, ask about the cases and what his or her opinions were. Beware if a witness had the exact opinion on both sides of an issue. You do not want an expert whom your opponent can prove is a hanging witness by constantly ruling that drivers are always at fault in the bike path case. You never know when your opposition may do the necessary research and find out this answer.

If you use an expert in your case, either by testimony or other means, you will need to lay the foundation for the expert by either questioning the witness — if he or she is present — on his or her background and expertise. Also, be precise: If you are entering written testimony of the person's résumé or CV to the court, prepare a verbal summarization as to why this expert has exactly the information necessary to answer the technical questions in your case.

SUMMARY

As the state-mandated upper limits of the small claims court system have increased, it has become increasingly popular to use expert witnesses to present technical details of your presentation. Case law for court-funded experts was developed from the federal level [Gates v. United States, 707 F.2d 1141 (10th Cir. 1983)] to distinguish the jobs of judges as law interpreters and expert witnesses as fact finders. This is done to the point where there will be increased use of experts who are either paid by the court or the judgment debtor above the otherwise established limits of the small claims court.

The real values of an expert witnesses are that they can testify, without personal experience on the specifics of the case. They can express their opinions when non experts have to stick to verifiable facts. Experts can testify to issues that would otherwise be inadmissible as evidence. An expert on cellular phone usage might be able to testify in our bike path case that talking on the cellular phone without a hands-free connection increases the risks of an automobile accident by 43 percent. Expert witnesses can also testify about pretrial disclosures by using the discovery material as data for specialized scientific analysis.

CHAPTER 11:

THE TRIAL DAY

Most of the text in previous chapters is designed to assist you in preparing for your trial day. If you do not visit the court to see how it works before your set a court date, then you will have miss an opportunity to learn how to interact with your judge. But, in this chapter, we will go through one case that has been developed to show you what the trial may be like. This is the bike path example, which includes a jury trial.

PRESENT YOUR CASE TO THE JUDGE

When most small claims court sessions begin, there is a mass oath and affirmation session. All who are expecting to give testimony in any case before the court that day will be asked to rise and affirm that they will tell the truth — the whole truth — before the court. A case, where either the plaintiff or defendant did not appear, is disposed of either through a default if the plaintiff is missing or by a default judgment to the plaintiff if the defendant is missing.

In larger jurisdictions, the court may be divided into groups, and cases are moved to separate courtrooms for a hearing by a judge other than the presiding judge who started the process. In jurisdictions where a mediation element is required before a case can be heard, a roll will be taken of those who still need to go to mediation, and those cases will start with a round of mediation. Trials scheduled for the use of a jury will also be separated to a different courtroom.

When your case is called, you will leave the gallery (audience area) and enter the trial area. This normally consists of two tables, one for each side, and the presence of any display devices or paraphernalia you asked the court clerk before the trial to provide. The judge in a small claims court may be on a raised bench as you would normally picture in a courtroom.

In a case with a judge and a jury, you need to begin your opening statement by addressing the judge by his or her name and then start with your rehearsed opening statement to both the judge and jury. Use your eyes to make contact with the judge, and then focus on a particular jury member when your eyes move in each person's direction.

In injury cases it is particularly advantageous to have a central drawing or picture to use in maintaining the jury's focus on the main issue of the case. In our example, you have a bicyclist struck in a bike path by an automobile. **Figure 11.1: Sample Attention Focus Exhibit** keeps the attention of all members of the court on the issue of the basic safety that a bike path is purposed to provide the bike rider.

After you have finished your opening statement, the other party may be able to present an opening statement (this varies from state to state). Although the traffic report indicated that the automobile entered the protected bike path, the countersuit claims that the bicycle moved into the traffic lane. This may conflict with your interview in which his witness implied that a bike path existed on this highway.

Whiteboard with Drawing of Sign Used to Slow Traffic on Bike Routes

Photo of Highway Marker near Accident Site (Right Side of Road)

FIGURE 11.3: SAMPLE AUTO ACCIDENT REPORT

Hawkins Police Report — Hasterton County

NAME: Driver 1: Keenan Williams

Address 114 Shady Lane, RR 6

City/State Coster, TN XXXXX

License #54-8275916

Driver 2: Carson Myer

Route 3, Box 733, Green Ferry Road

Coster, TN XXXXX

License #98-1121654

Injuries: Driver 2, the bicyclist, was transported to Hawkins Municipal Hospital with apparent injuries to his right leg and right arm.

Vehicle Information:

Vehicle 1 Tag: THB 1561 Year: 20XX   Make: Ford   Model: Explorer

Vehicle 2 N/A   Year: 20XX   Make: N/A   Model: Mountain Bike

Damage: Bicycle was totaled, with both wheels bent and broken and lightweight frame bent. Auto had minor paint damage to front impact bumper.

Drawing of Accident: Indicate cars by drivers' numbers above: (Initial here, and sign below.)

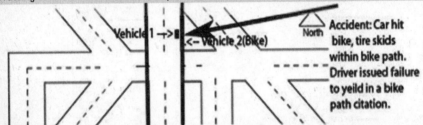

Accident Information: Date: 4/19/20XX Time: 15:30 Vehicle 1 Passengers 1: 2. Vehicle 2 Passengers: 1.

Description: Driver 1 moved into restricted bicycle lane and hit Driver 2, the bicyclist. The tire marks indicated an attempt to stop AFTER the other vehicle (bike) was struck. A "moving" citation was issued to Vehicle 1's driver for failing to yield in a bike bath. Four photos were taken of accident after transport of Driver 2 to hospital. No passengers in Vehicle 1 complained of any injuries. A second citation was issued for failure to carry the required auto insurance.

FIGURE 11.3: SAMPLE AUTO ACCIDENT REPORT

Witness Information:	Address:	Phone:
Marie Gerstat (Car following Vehicle 1)	471 Hall/Hawkins	XXX-XXX-XXXX
Thomas Jelus (Walker on opposite curb)	512 Mark/Coster	XXX-XXX-XXXX

Other Information:_____

_____

Reported by: Officer: Hank Quinn Badge: 443 Signature: *Hank Quinn*

NOTICE: Section 72 of the Penal Code provides "Every person who, with intent to defraud, presents for allowance or for payment to any state or local officer, verbally or in writing, is guilty of a felony."   Revised: 9/20XX

KEEP THE PRESENTATION LOGICAL

As you start your presentation with evidence and witnesses, hand out copies to the jury of **Figure 11.2: Sample Photo Exhibit**, then explain that this marker was near the accident. Emphasize that the auto driver must have passed it just before the accident. Use your presentation card, **Figure 9.5: Sample Analysis of Evidence Card**, to point to the yield sign that was close to the accident site. Impress on the jury that there are hundreds of bike paths in the state that are built to precise safety standards to protect both the auto driver and the bike rider.

The next logical piece of evidence would be the police report. At this phase, you should have a copy for the judge and one to be passed around to the jury; the defendant should have been told how to obtain the report at the time of the accident. Point out to the jury that there were two witnesses to the case. Also, indicate that your opponent was issued two traffic citations. The failure to carry the minimum liability insurance shows disregard of the law. The citation for failure to yield to a bike rider in a bike path establishes responsibility for your injuries and other losses.

After you have completed the evidence presentation phase, you can interview your witness using the questions on **Figure 9.4: Sample Questioning of Witness Card**. As we know from the previous chapter, the witness is expected to testify that the automobile driver was talking on his cellular phone in an agitated manner, rather than paying attention to his driving performance.

The procedures vary from state to state. In some states, you will give your closing statement and allow the other side to present its case. In other states, you may rest your case to allow the other side to present its case. Whichever is allowed, it is best to wait to close after the other case is presented completely. This offers you the opportunity to cross-examine all witnesses.

BE PREPARED FOR ANY UNEXPECTED EVENT

In the bike path case, your interview with the other witness has told you to expect a different story than that from your witness. You must always be ready for unexpected events. Witnesses viewing the same event will often come away with different conclusions; often, their point of view may tell a different story. In this situation, the other witness — a driver who was riding behind the accident automobile — did not see the cellular phone in use nor the supposed swerve of the bike into the auto's path. She did not see, as would be expected, the driver of the car moving into the bike lane.

Using your strategy developed on your cue card, **Figure 9.6: Sample Cross-examination Questions Card**, you should be able to slowly change the impact of this witness. Move from question to question, at first asking a question that hardly seems to matter, only to find that it leads to a question that turns the testimony around 180 degrees. In the end, you may have moved the testimony from one that favors the opponent to one that — at worst — was neutral.

TRY TO FOLLOW YOUR PLAN

Bring all evidence to the court in presentable condition. Make the documents as large as possible if you have a jury present. Make your presentation seem uniform. If necessary, use the professionals of a copy center to do it right. Present documents that show what an expert witness would have shown, even if you did not use one. Have a pointer available in at least two sizes: one for the easel and other for 8.5-by-11-inch documents so that you can show the judge and jury what you are talking about.

Arrive at court early so you do not lose by a default judgment. Your case likely will not be the first, so be patient. Present your opening statement in a thoughtful and serious manner. Allow the opposition to interact in the case as it progresses. The judge will determine if he or she is out of order. Do not make statements to the opposition directly. All of your presentation should be addressed to the judge and the jury if one is present. Avoid displays of emotion in any part of the trial. If the judge asks questions, answer them as distinctly as possible.

If something occurs in the testimony or evidence presented, try to carefully evaluate its impact on your case before you react emotionally. If the information supplied in court was not available to you before court, in most cases you can get a continuance until a later date. It is better not to do this in small claims court because you will have to start your case from the beginning. Like most civil courts, rules of discovery require that both sides supply information about their proposed case in advance.

FIGURE 11.4: TRANSCRIPT OF JUDGMENT

Case # 171-887498-0

Judgment CREDITOR
Michael J. Miller, Pres.
Professional Services, Inc.
121 Broadway
Houston, GA XXXXX
(XXX) XXX-XXXX

FIGURE 11.4: TRANSCRIPT OF JUDGMENT

Judgment DEBTOR

Acme Janitorial

1401 14th Street

Cowin, GA XXXXX

JURISDICTION COURT

Superior Court of Hennpenny County

Superior Court Square, Room 101

Oakdale, GA XXXXX

Small Claims Branch

For the Use of the Court Only

Transcript of Judgment
Hennpenny Chief Clerk for Superior Court of Hennpenny County

1. Amount of judgment as follows:

a. Damages awarded	$ 1,784.97
b. Costs	$ 250.00
c. Prospective fees	$ 40.00
TOTAL	$ 2,074.97

2. I, __Jack Abehr__, Chief Clerk of the Superior Court of Hennpenny County, Small Claims Division, hereby certify that the above is true and correct Transcript of Judgment for the case number listed above and in the records of my office. I hereby sign this transcript this __14__ day of __July__, 20XX.

Date: __7/14/20XX__   Signed: __Jack Abehr__

3. A copy of this Transcript of Judgment was mailed to both the creditor and debtor listed above at the addresses shown above this date and recorded below as an official instrument of this office.

County	Date of Recording	Instrument Number
Hennpenny	6/13/20XX	14-7678-983

NOTICE TO THE Judgment DEBTOR: If this Transcript of Judgment is incorrect in any material way, you have 10 calendar days to notify this office and petition the court for a correction of this judgment. Judgments not so challenged shall stand as correct under the laws of the state, regardless of the court's decision in the above-numbered case.

PRESENTATION OF AN EXPERT WITNESS

If you are presenting expert testimony, either through an expert witness who is present in the courtroom or by letter as shown in **Figure 10.3: Expert Witness Testimony by Letter**, you should select the moment of greatest impact to do so. Normally, you should use the expert as your last witness before the opposition gives their testimony. Present the expert's credentials first and their evidentiary points will follow.

If the expert is going to testify to something that will rebut an opposition witness, you should wait until the opposition has completed its case and you have done your cross-examination to introduce the expert witness as a rebuttal witness. In the bike path case, the expert testimony reports that regardless of what the other witnesses said, the tire track evidence shows that there was no braking of the Explorer before the impact with the bicycle. The automobile driver is at fault through pure scientific evidence and not testimony that was biased by their visual perspective of the accident itself.

THE JUDGMENT

As shown in **Figure 11.4: Transcript of Judgment**, you should not expect the judge's decision to be something you can hang on your wall to represent a battle well fought and won. A judgment is about money. The judgment will contain the information the court requires to maintain its records and the information both parties need to go forward after trial. The judgment is sometimes presented at the end of the trial, and in other cases it is taken under advisement for later action. In the latter case, you will either get the judgment in the mail or have to pick it up at the court clerk's office.

SUMMARY

This chapter has summarized the trial process using an example case. You should now know your responsibilities, no matter which side you are representing in the court. The judge may set rules for the presentation of the case that are different from those presented in this chapter. That is why you should visit the court before the actual trial date. Now, you should have a good idea on how you present or defend your case.

CHAPTER 12:

ALL IS NOT LOST IF YOUR OPPONENT WINS

After the trial has been completed, you will receive the court's decision. Small claims court decisions are not final; therefore, you can always appeal the decision. Note that this is a two-way street. Occasionally, the decision you like will be one that your opponent cannot accept. This is the nature of the dispute process. If you could have resolved it between yourselves, you would not have gone to court.

It is not a requirement that you have countersued or filed counterclaims to obtain an appeal path available to you. If you feel the decision was not totally correct, you may file with the court for a rehearing, retrial, or transfer to a higher court where the decision of the small claims court can be overruled. The appeal's process will take extra time, and most cases will not be overturned.

IF YOU LOSE, FIGHT BACK

Even if there is a clerical error in the judgment, you should file with the court to make the judgment correct. **Figure 12.1: Sample Motion to Modify Judgment** shows a typical request of a motion to make a clerical correction to the judgment. Judgments can have incorrect case damage amounts, failures to allow for approved costs, or simple mathematical errors. Filing this type of motion will compel the corrected judgment to be prepared and returned to both parties within a few days.

FIGURE 12.1: SAMPLE MOTION TO MODIFY JUDGMENT

Civil Court of the City of Monroe

Small Claims Division

_____

In the Matter of

                                            Motion to Modify Judgment

    Joseph A. Bask   (Attach Debtor Judgment)

         v.

    Kelly Anne Morton   Case # XX-XXXXX-X _____

The Judgment Creditor, Joseph A. Bask , does hereby petition the court, with service to the Judgment Debtor, Kelly Anne Morton, for a Motion to Modify the judgment incorrectly entered as follows:

A judgment incorrectly recorded as to the amount as follows:

a. Damages awarded	$ 784.97
b. Costs	$ 250.00
c. Prospective fees	$ 40.00
TOTAL	$ 1,074.97

When the correct Judgment amount should be as follows:

a. Damages awarded	$ 1,784.97
b. Costs	$ 250.00
c. Prospective fees	$ 40.00
TOTAL	$ 2,074.97

Executed this date: 1/30/20XX

Joseph A. Bask
_____
Joseph A. Bask, Plaintiff, Pro se

Joseph A. Bask

141 Yellow Brick Road

Monroe, TX XXXXX

If you want to appeal the decision, you may do so at the small claims court clerk's office. In some cases, the small claims court will have a retrial. In other states, your appeal may be handled in the civil court division. **Figure 12.2: Sample Notice of Appeal** shows an example form to use in starting an appeal to the next higher court in your state. You can continue to appeal until you have the decision you want or you go to the Supreme Court.

You will notice that the request for an appeal is quite simple. The information requested is no more than an affirmation that you desire the appeal. You may be asked to pay additional fees, and you will have to serve notice of the appeal application to the other parties of the suit. The clerk may allow you to notify the other parties by certified mail, but in some jurisdictions the service must meet the same rigorous standards as the original case.

The appeal to be reheard in the small claims court can be scheduled to suit your needs if you visit the court clerk's office. However, appeals to a higher court may be harder to set at a convenient date for you. Most civil courts have heavy calendars, and working in your appeal may take some time. The court will give appropriate required legal notice for your state, but you may not be able to control the trial date.

FIGURE 12.2: SAMPLE NOTICE OF APPEAL

Civil Court of the City of Monroe

Small Claims Division

_____

In the Matter of

    Joseph A. Bask

      v.

    Kelly Anne Morton

Notice of Appeal
(Attach Debtor Judgment)

Case # XX-XXXXX-X

_____ Please take notice that the above named ☑Plaintiff __Defendant hereby appeal(s) to THE APPELLATE TERM OF THE SUPREME COURT from the decision of the Small Claims Division of the Civil Division of the Court of the City of Monroe. In this action, official notice of the Small Claims Court decision was entered in the office of the Clerk of the Court on the __7__ day of __January, 20XX__, and

FIGURE 12.3: SAMPLE APPEAL DECISION

from every part thereof an appeal is hereby made.

This notice of appeal was served on the _Plaintiff ☑Defendant at the address of record as follows: 1471 Hill Street, Monroe, TX XXXXX.

Yours, etc.

Joseph A. Bask
_____

  Joseph A. Bask, Plaintiff, Pro se

Joseph A. Bask
141 Yellow Brick Road

Monroe, TX XXXXX   At a term of the Appellate Term of the
                              Supreme Court of the State of New York
CASE # XX-XXXXX B C   for the 2nd and 11th Judicial Districts
January 13, 20XX TERM   held in Bronx County on January 23, 20XX.
PRESENT" HON. BERNARD JONES,   JUSTICE PRESIDING
   "   HON. MARIE KELLY,   ASSOCIATE JUSTICE
   "   HON. KATHERINE MILLER,   ASSOCIATE JUSTICE
---x
JULIOUS HENRY
               Appellant
JANICE WHITE
               Respondent
---x

The above named appellant, having appealed to this court for a Judgment of the CIVIL COURT OF THE CITY OF NEW YORK, BRONX COUNTY entered on July 12, 20XX, and said appeal having been submitted by APPELLANT IN PERSON and NO BRIEF SUBMITTED for the respondent and due deliberation having been had thereon; It is hereby ordered and adjudicated that the Judgment is unanimously reversed without cost.

JULIOUS HENRY
35 CASTER STREET
BRONX, NY XXXXX

Jaclyn A. Behr

FIGURE 12.3: SAMPLE APPEAL DECISION	
JANICE WHITE	
141 HARRIS COURT	JACLYN A. BEHR
BRONX, NY XXXXX	CHIEF CLERK
	APPELLATE TERM

You should visit the higher court and watch the proceedings as you did in the small claims court. You will find most cases are handled by attorneys. The clerk of this court can tell you when a similar small claims appeal will be heard.

APPEAL OR SECOND TRIAL

Your first appeal may take you before the same court, and, possibly, the same judge, that previously gave you an adverse decision. If this will be the case, you should redouble your efforts to present an effective case. Call witnesses whom you did not contact in the first trial, present better exhibits, or get an expert witness to explain issues you think the court failed to fully understand.

Because there is a time limit on when you can appeal a small claims court case, you may wish to work on the case and its presentation until the last date for appeal. When you have met the deadline, you will have a fixed period before the case is retried. Be sure the case is not a rehash of the old presentation. If your witnesses and evidence are the same, work on your presentations, reorganize the order you use in presenting the evidence, and take advantage of your opponent's weaknesses in the first trial against him.

You may find that a retrial in small claims court ends with the same decision. In most states, then you can move the case to a higher court. In these courts, presentations by an attorney is the norm. Once again you should visit trials of similar cases to get the feel of how to deal with the facts and witnesses. You will have a fresh judge in your next court appearance, therefore, you should have a fair hearing based on facts and law. **Figure 12.3: Sample Appeal Decision** shows a typical decision of a state supreme court to reverse the actions of a small claims court. In cases where the higher courts simply reverse the lower court's decision, you may have to return to the lower court to get a judgment with an amount you can collect from your opponent.

DOUBLE JEOPARDY

You must remember that your opponent has the right to be free of double jeopardy. Here, this means that you must follow the state's approved appeals process to the letter. So long as the civil case is in litigation, double jeopardy does not attach, even if you appeal all the way to the highest court within your state. If you do this, you should always go to visit the court to see other cases being presented before you have your case appealed there. This will allow you to understand the different formats each court uses.

SUMMARY

The small claims court system, like all other courts in the United States, has an appeal course to seek a rehearing of the issues before a different decision maker if the decision does not go your way.

Although your rehearing can be in the same small claims court where you previously lost, most states allow you then to move into the civil court system. This can lead you to the Supreme Court of your state or the U.S. Supreme Court, if you are willing to fight the case that far. Appeals are often only reversed in cases where there is a legal issue at stake. It is rare for the higher courts to hear the entire evidentiary case again after it has been heard in small claims court.

If you have a case that includes reliance on case law, it may take a higher court to agree with your contention that the facts of your case match the facts of the case law to have a new hearing based on evidence to support these issues. As with any case, it is important that you do your homework in the beginning. You should know not only what the law says in light of your dispute but what previous decisions have shown that should be your outcome.

CHAPTER 13:

APPROACHING THE DEFENDANT FOR PAYMENT

If the judge signs the court's decision and gives you the judgment in court, which is frequently the case, you should start trying to collect from the judgment debtor immediately. There is a psychological advantage to getting a commitment from the other party before you leave the courthouse. Debtors often become inaccessible as soon as they leave the court. They may also change their attitudes about paying you; therefore, it is in your best interest to make getting payment a primary goal before the debtor steps beyond the court's doors.

TRY COLLECTING RIGHT AWAY

You can suggest that the easy way to resolve the debt might be through payments the debtor makes into a court-administered escrow account. Check in advance for the requirements, and, if necessary, prepare a partially filled-out request to the court similar to that in **Figure 13.1: Sample Agreement for Court to Escrow Settlement**. If the court does not receive the funds, the debtor can be found in contempt if he or she does not keep the agreement. It offers affordable payments if the judgment is considerably large for the debtor to pay in one lump sum.

FIGURE 13.1: SAMPLE AGREEMENT FOR COURT TO ESCROW SETTLEMENT

Civil Court of the City of Monroe

Small Claims Division

In the Matter of

Joseph A. Bask

v.

Kelly Anne Morton

Petition to Establish
Escrowed Payments
with the Court and to
Establish Times and Terms
(Attach Debtor Judgment)

The Judgment Creditor, _Joseph A. Bask_ , does hereby petition the court, with service to the Judgment Debtor, _Kelly Anne Morton_ , for the establishment of an escrow account with the court on terms as follows:

1. The Judgment entered per the attached action finds that the Judgment Debtor owes _$2,311.43_ to the Judgment Creditor, and with this petition the Judgment Creditor does hereby request that the court collect and escrow the funds from the Judgment Debtor for the Judgment Creditor.

2. The Judgment shall be paid in _six_ equal payments of _$385.24_ . Each payment is to be due on the 25th day of each month, starting with the initial payment due 6/25/20XX.

3. There shall be ☑ No☐Yes: a _____day grace period.

4. If the payment is more than ten days late, a late fee of ten percent of the balance still owed, plus a $25 court administration fee, shall be additionally due.

5. If the Judgment Debtor is late more than three times in the payment period or misses two consecutive payments, he or she shall be considered in contempt of the court, and the court shall administer other just and reasonable measures.

6. The Judgment Creditor has assigned this debt to an agent or collection agency as defined under state law. This agency is:

FIGURE 13.1: SAMPLE AGREEMENT FOR COURT TO ESCROW SETTLEMENT

_____. The agency shall receive the sums escrowed under this judgment as if it were the Judgment Creditor.

I declare under penalty of perjury under the laws of this state that the foregoing is true and correct.

Joseph A. Bask   , Judgment Creditor

_____, Collection Agent for the Judgment Creditor

Attach Assignment or Appointment as Agent

NOTICE TO THE Judgment DEBTOR

If you dispute any allegation made on this Petition, you must file a declaration in opposition to the Petition with the Small Claims Court within ten days of the mailing of this Petition.

FIGURE 13.2: REQUEST TO SET ASIDE PAYMENTS WITH TERMS

Civil Court of the City of Monroe

Small Claims Division

_____

In the Matter of

Joseph A. Bask

v.

Kelly Anne Morton

_____

Petition to Establish
Set Aside Payments
with the Payment Creditor and to
Establish Times and Terms
(Attach Debtor Judgment)

The Judgment Creditor, Joseph A. Bask , does hereby petition the court, with service to the Judgment Debtor, Kelly Anne Morton , for the establishment of a fixed payment plan with the sanction of the court on the terms as follows:

1. The Judgment entered per the attached action finds that the Judgment Debtor owes $2,311.43 to the Judgment Creditor, and with this petition, the Judgment Creditor does hereby request that funds from the Judgment Debtor be made to the Judgment Creditor through an established agent as established herein.

FIGURE 13.2: REQUEST TO SET ASIDE PAYMENTS WITH TERMS

2. The Judgment shall be paid in _six_ equal payments of _$385.24_ . Each payment is to be due on the 25th day of each month, starting with the initial payment due 6/25/20XX.

3. There shall be ☑No☐Yes: a ____day grace period.

4. If the payment is more than ten days late, a late fee of ten percent of the balance still owed, plus a $25 administration fee shall be additionally due.

5. If the Judgment Debtor is late more than three times in the payment period or misses two consecutive payments, he or she may be considered in contempt of the court, and if the Judgment Creditor requests, the Court may administer other just and reasonable measures.

6. The Judgment Creditor has assigned this debt to an agent or collection agency as defined under state law. This agency is: _Acme Universal Collections._ The agency shall receive the sums under this judgment as if it were the Judgment Creditor.

I declare under penalty of perjury under the laws of this state that the foregoing is true and correct.

_____ , Judgment Creditor

_____*Rubin Jell*____ , Collection Agent for the Judgment Creditor

Attach Assignment or Appointment as Agent

NOTICE TO THE Judgment DEBTOR

If you dispute any allegation made on this Petition, you must file a declaration in opposition to the Petition with the Small Claims Court within ten days of the mailing of this Petition.

FIGURE 13.3: SAMPLE AGREEMENT TO SATISFY JUDGMENT WITH TERMS

Jimmy Dukes
1480 Burnside Road
Cabot Hills, NH XXXXX

July 12, 20XX

Mr. Henry Thames
Executive Director
Rural Transportation Agency
Banner Courthouse Annex
Generosity, NH XXXXX

Subject: Proposed Agreement to Satisfy Judgment with Terms

Dear Mr. Thames,

I, Jimmy Dukes, declare as follows:

1. I have a judgment against the Rural Transportation Agency from the Small Claims Division of the Superior Court of Generosity (Case # 1221-122).

2. Because you have verbally indicated that there are no funds in the agency's budget for the judgment, I desire to have the judgment paid to me over time to meet your funds' availability as is available under the state's statutes for payment with terms.

3. The exact amount of the judgment is $2,415.00 (with accrued interest from the judgment date of 2/23/20XX), and I will accept monthly payments for up to 24 months at the legal maximum interest rate of ten percent per year.

I declare under penalty of perjury under the laws of the state that the foregoing is true and correct.

Offered by: Accepted by:

Jimmy Dukes   *Henry Thames*

Jimmy Dukes   Henry Thames
Judgment Creditor   Judgment Debtor for
                                                     Rural Transportation Agency

This petition to establish payments and have them escrowed in an account with the court is simple to fill out. Normally, the judgment creditor can simply obtain the form, have it typed, and turn it back to the court clerk for a fee. The clerk has all the authority necessary to establish the account because the judgment has already been entered and recorded in his or her office. The example in **Figure 13.1** illustrates how to set up six monthly payments to settle the total debt. It allows for there to be no grace period on the date the payment is due each month — in this case, the 25th day of each month. If the judgment debtor assigns the debt to a credit agency, the credit agent signs the form in place of the judgment creditor and attaches his or her authority to act for the judgment creditor.

In some states, the court can also sanction an agreement to contract for repayment with fixed monthly payments and a set interest rate. Although this does not have the kind of psychological persuasion as a court escrow account, the presence of possible contempt of court may be precisely what you need to get the judgment paid. An example of this type of court-sanctioned agreement between the judgment creditor and judgment debtor is shown as **Figure 13.2: Request to Set Aside Payments with Terms**.

This form is a simple transfer of debt ownership from the judgment creditor of record with the court to his or her designated credit agency. Because the funds are being paid directly to the credit agency, it will normally start calling, or, otherwise, make the late payment known to the court. The court can be asked to have the debtor examined to determine why he or she has missed a payment or where there are currently assets that can be attached or garnisheed to complete the established payment program.

You can also prepare your own agreement to present to the judgment debtor after court such as the one shown in **Figure 13.3: Sample Agreement to Satisfy Judgment with Terms**. This kind of agreement is especially helpful when the judgment debtor is finding it difficult to pay off the debt. Getting an agreement to pay it as soon as possible reinforces your judgment if you later need to go to court to obtain the funds or hire a collection service to secure payment.

The letter should spell out the names and addresses of both parties and have a place for both to sign, agreeing to the terms. It should reference the case, either by number or name, and include the total amount of the judgment debt. It should include the amount of the debt and the applicable interest rate, if any, that will accrue after a given date. If monthly payments are provided, as a minimum there should be a final date or period when the debt is expected to be paid off in full.

FIGURE 13.4: COMPROMISE AGREEMENT

Settlement Agreement

THIS IS AN AGREEMENT BETWEEN Carlos Mantise, the party of the first part, AND Mario Hughes, the party of the second part:

WHEREAS, there has been a disagreement about $4,000 owed the party of the first part by the party of the second part for some time. This agreement is intended to settle the disagreement by a compromise where neither party admits fault or guilt with regard to the underlying debt.

THE PARTIES HEREBY AGREE AS FOLLOWS:

1. The party of the second part will pay the party of the first part $3,500 within 72 hours of the signing of this agreement.

2. The party of the second part shall have no further liability or obligation to the party of the first part in connection with any past debts for services rendered.

3. No additional payments shall be required to be paid or transferred to the party of the first part from the party of the second part.

4. The nature and effect of this agreement is to extinguish the obligations, heretofore, between them arising out of this past disagreement and/or written or verbal contract.

5. This agreement shall not be treated as an admission of liability by either party for any purpose, or be admissible as evidence before any tribunal or court.

FIGURE 13.4: COMPROMISE AGREEMENT

6. This compromise, hereby, releases and discharges both parties from any further obligation under this disagreement. This compromise settles any and all past, present, or future claims, demands, or obligations whether based on tort, contract, or other theories of recovery. The parties may not assign any obligation from the other party in interest to heirs or assigns.

7. The parties acknowledge and agree that upon execution of the release, this agreement applies to all claims for damages or losses either party may have against the other whether those damages or losses are known or unknown, foreseen or unforeseen.

IN WITNESS WHEREOF, the parties and signatories execute this agreement on the date indicated.

Date Signed:_____

_____

Carlos Mantise, Master Carpenter, Inc., Creditor, and Party of the first part.

_____

Mario Hughes, Inc., General Contractor, Debtor and Party of the second part.

If the judgment debtor has a local bank account check, you might offer to accept payment in the check and mark the debtor's copy of the judgment as paid by check, citing the bank and check number. If the check proves not to have funds to back it up, keep the bounced check as your proof that the debt remains unpaid. Today's latest electronic banking statements often fail to show a large picture of the bounced check, but you can get a copy by requesting it at your local branch.

COMPROMISE TO GET QUICK PAYMENT

If there does not appear to be any way to get your judgment debtor to pay on the courthouse steps, you might consider offering a compromise agreement similar to the agreement shown as **Figure 13.4: Compromise Agreement**. In a compromise agreement such as this, there is a grace period (in this instance, it is 72 hours) for the debtor to get certified funds to pay the judgment creditor. The last thing you want to do is agree to a lesser amount without being absolutely sure the funds will be good. Do not accept personal or business checks when you compromise. You brought a discount to the table, and the debtor needs to bring cash or certified funds.

If an agreement is a compromise, it should mention the fact that the dispute was for a larger amount and that the parties have settled for a lower amount that is to be paid within the terms of the contract. Also, the contract should say that it becomes invalid if the terms on which you agreed do not occur as spelled out in the agreement. It should list the full and complete names of the parties and their relationship. The contract should specifically release the parties from any further liabilities of the compromise if it is completed with payment as outlined.

SUMMARY

Those familiar with small claims court cases know that the hardest part of your work will come after the court has ruled in your favor. The ideas and exhibits in this chapter are designed to make winning your final game. These tactics are less effective if you do not walk out of the courtroom with a signed judgment, but they can be used later if you can keep in contact with your debtor.

Collection of the judgment becomes a much bigger problem with large judgments. Try to focus the debtor's mind on ways to pay the judgment more easily. Permitting him or her to pay less is one way and letting the debtor pay over time is another. Be prepared in advance with one or more forms that you can use to agree to payment over time, or pay a lesser amount with the debtor's quick delivery of cash.

CHAPTER 14:

FINDING ASSETS

As you prepare for the case, you may find that your opponent is going to be difficult to serve. It might even be a bigger problem to collect. When collection looks as though it may be a chore, you should approach the clerk's office and determine what court assistance you can get in assuring payment after a judgment is made. Many states allow for a debtor examination procedure, either as part of the case service process or as an aspect of the trial itself.

HAVING THE COURT HELP YOU COLLECT

If your state is one of those that offers assistance, you need to prepare paperwork that will allow the court to do the job necessary in collecting the potential debt. **Figure 14.1: Sample Debtor's Statement of Assets** shows a subpoena that the court can issue to ask the defendant in a case to submit financial information. If the decision grants the plaintiff a judgment, the court will use the information to question the defendant in open court about his or her finances. You will need to take notes because the actual form data may not be given to you, even if the judgment is in your favor. Always keep a notepad and some pens at your fingertips at court.

The forms identify five kinds of assets. First are jobs or other sources of income that can be used to pay the judgment. If the judgment debtor is unwilling to pay your claim directly, you can have the funds collected at the wage source through a process called garnishment. In this scenario, the court — or in some states the sheriff — can send an order to the employer to pay the debtor's wages directly to the judgment creditor.

In some cases, a certain living wage must still be paid to the actual wage earner so only part of the employee's net wages are used to pay the debt. Although this seems like a good method to use in collecting a debt, if the debt takes more than a few pay periods to be paid off, employees often find other jobs where they can have their full take-home pay. The judgment creditor, in this situation, is left to find the new job location and start the process over.

Second, a Statement of Assets form, as in **Figure 14.1,** will identify real assets (real estate) on which you could place a lien if necessary. This is an extremely effective collection method but not a fast method to use in collecting a judgment debt. The real property cannot be sold, refinanced, or otherwise have the title changed until the lien is paid off along with any accumulated interest. Normally, interest accrues on all judgment debts at a state-mandated maximum amount. It compounds annually and can grow substantially over time.

The single-family home is bought or sold on an average of about once every three years. This means that on average, the lien can be expected to be cleared within the three years. This is not a guarantee, but the property will never have a clear title until this lien is paid to the judgment creditor.

Next listed on the Statement of Assets will be any owned automobiles on which you might place a lien. If the vehicles are owned free and clear of any loans, they can be seized. Because the average American buys automobiles on time payments of more than $450 per month, most cars are not worth more than the debt already on the car's title within the first year of ownership. Large judgment debts are not likely to be satisfied by seizing and selling a car listed as an asset.

Finally, the Statement of Assets will identify bank deposits and other valuable property that you may be able to have the court acquire. Bank assets offer the best source of funds for recovering a judgment. Some judgment debtors will have retirement accounts that the court can require be sold with the proceeds being used to pay off the judgment debt. Assets such as boats, recreational vehicles, or all-terrain vehicles are likely to be worth little due to the loans on them.

If you have the court obtain a list of assets of the judgment debtor, the simple fact that he or she has been forced to give you this information may have a positive effect on his or her desire to quickly pay off what the court says that you are owed.

FIGURE 14.1: SAMPLE DEBTOR'S STATEMENT OF ASSETS

Municipal Court San Bernardino   JT1210-1221

Name and address of Court: Claims Case Number: Small

44191 Sage Highway, Joshua Tree, CA XXXXX

Judgment DEBTOR'S STATEMENT OF ASSETS
SMALL CLAIMS COURT SUBPOENA

EMPLOYMENT

1. I, the undersigned debtor defendant, declare that I have the following employment:

A. Employer: Dairy Bell Ice Cream Delivery (weekly) Martin's Stop 'N Go, Cashier (Part-Time Daily)

123 Cardiff Way, Desert View, CA XXXXX 7th & A Streets, Desert View, CA XXXXX

B. If not employed, list other forms of income.

C. How often are you paid?

☑ daily ☐ every two weeks ☐ monthly

☑ weekly ☐ twice a week ☐ Other (Explain):_____

SELF: NET per pay period:_____ (take-home pay)
GROSS per pay period _____
SPOUSE: NET per pay period:_____ (take-home pay)
GROSS per pay period _____

FIGURE 14.1: SAMPLE DEBTOR'S STATEMENT OF ASSETS

CASH BANK DEPOSITS

2. I have the following money in cash:_____

a. List bank name, address, account number, and amount for each on the back of this sheet as "ANSWER TO QUESTION 2a."

REAL PROPERTY

3. I own real estate. ☑Yes — List below ☐No

      a. Home, 1411 Arboleda Street, Yuba City, CA XXXXX

      b.

      c.

AUTOMOBILE PROPERTY

4. I, the undersigned debtor defendant, declare that I have the following automobiles not used as my only means for getting to work. ☑None ☐two cars ☐ three or more cars. List all including license and location of place garaged on back as "ANSWER TO QUESTION 4."

Other Personal Property

5. I have listed on back all other property owned, valued at $50 or more as "ANSWER TO QUESTION 5."

I declare, under penalty of perjury under the laws of this state, that the foregoing is true and correct.

Date Signed: **May 20, 20XX** Defendant ___*John Smith*___

In some states, the small claims court subpoena powers will allow you to obtain asset information from third parties, particularly in bad check cases. In these circumstances, you may have information on where the person has recently kept a bank account. In some states, you may gather information from him or her under the court's subpoena powers before the trial.

If this is available and you have an idea where a bank asset exists, subpoena the branch manager of the bank to have him or her supply information as in **Figure 14.2: Question and Answer Information Subpoena**. If you are located in a small rural area with few banking institutions, the court may allow you to subpoena all officials to supply helpful facts. Information that you obtain through these subpoenas is likely exempt from any discovery rules, as they do not relate directly to the case and could be used only as a collection method after a judgment is granted.

As we will see later, there are a number of ways to seek information on assets after the judgment is in hand. A few states allow this to be done along with the collection of other information. In cases where the trial judge is going to have to rule on whom is at fault, this kind of information is not available. When the issue is simply the amount of money due, the court is more flexible in gathering financial information. It often lessens the court's workload to accumulate collection information early, and most often you can use these tools when it is a bad check or bad debt case. The probative value of the information is often necessary when the judgment debtor simply claims he or she has no assets or funds to pay.

FIGURE 14.2: QUESTION AND ANSWER INFORMATION SUBPOENA

Civil Court of the City of Monroe

Small Claims Division

In the Matter of

	Questions and Answers
Joseph A. Bask	in connection with an
v.	Informational Subpoena
Kelly Anne Morton	(Add attachments as necessary)

The City of Monroe, Small Claims Court, hereby orders you to answer the following questions and return this questionnaire information SUBPOENA to the person listed below:

Questions For: Judgment Debtor, <u>Kelly Anne Morton</u>

FIGURE 14.2: QUESTION AND ANSWER INFORMATION SUBPOENA

1. Q: Please provide the debtor's full name as indicated in your records.
A: Kelly A. Morton

2. Q: Please set forth the last known address and telephone number for the debtor's residence and work address:
A: Home: 1471 Hill Street; Work: 58 Monroe Industrial Park, both in Monroe, NO PHONE.

3. Q: Does the judgment debtor have an account with you, and are you currently holding any funds or securities? If so, what is the account number and the current balance?
A: Account 21-7865783-1, a savings account with a balance of $21,993.51.

4. Q: Do your records indicate that the debtor is employed? If so, please provide the employer's name and address.
A: Manner's Mills, 58 Monroe Industrial Park.

5. Q: Did the debtor list any bank references on his/her application? If so, please list said banks.
A: None.

6. Q: Do your records indicate the location of any other assets the debtor may own? If so, please provide the location and description of these assets.
A: We show a home loan on the 1471 Hill Street address.

Deliver to (Via SASE): Joseph A. Bask　Signed by: *Clarkson Dickerson*
　　141 Yellow Brick Road　　　　　　　For/Served: Master Monopoly Bank
　　Monroe, TX XXXXX　　　　　　　　　1 Bank Street
　　　　　　　　　　　　　　　　　　　　Monroe, TX XXXXX

SUMMARY

This chapter is designed to help you start the collection process for your judgment as soon as the court judgment has been issued. The single best time to have the judgment debtor and judgment creditor meet and establish a payment schedule at the courthouse itself. As soon as both parties move away from this physical location, it may be harder to get closure to the case and disputed issues.

You should always assume that you will win the judgment and have it solidified as soon as you leave the court's trial room. Be prepared with as much information on your opponent as possible, and try to get your payment that day. Have an alternative solution if you cannot get all your judgment right away. Be prepared to offer time payments or a discount to speed your judgment debtor's decision to pay you and end the aggravation of a continued dispute.

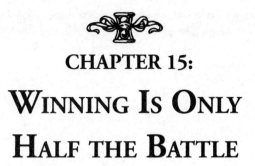

CHAPTER 15:

WINNING IS ONLY HALF THE BATTLE

The national average for collections of judgment debts suggests that 79 percent of the cases will never be collected. More than half of these uncollected debts were against judgment-proof debtors. If you follow the suggestions given in this book concerning different kinds of disputes, you may have a much better chance of recovering the debt the court awarded to you. No matter whether you are the original plaintiff or defendant, your chances of collecting will improve only if you make a concerted effort in the system to collect what is owed to you.

NECESSARY COLLECTION PAPERWORK

This chapter focuses on ways to collect your debt by primarily putting collection pressure on the judgment debtor directly. In the next chapter, we shall take up legal means of using the court's power to assist you in enforcing the judgment. Your efforts on the courthouse steps should have been firm but friendly. When this fails, you may find the solution lends itself to only much harsher measures.

After you have failed to get your funds on the courthouse steps, you should start, as you did with demand letters earlier, to write the judgment debtor and ask for payments. In **Figure 15.1: Sample Payment Request Letter**, you will find a way to start your assault on the judgment debtor. The letter should be professional yet cordial. It should exude your intention to fight for your funds, even if it is a long battle.

FIGURE 15.1: SAMPLE PAYMENT REQUEST LETTER

Melvin Peterson
13561 Golf Course Green
Louisville, KS XXXXX

April 10, 20XX

Mercer Martin
1441 Main Street
St. Louis, KS XXXXX
Re: Small Claims Case XXXX-XXXX-X

Dear Mr. Martin,

As you know, a judgment was entered in the above case number in Small Claims Court on April 20, 20XX in the amount of $2,175.00. As the judgment creditor, I would appreciate your paying the amount within ten days.

Thank you, in advance, for your attention to this matter.

Sincerely,

Melvin Peterson

Melvin Peterson

CC: Chief Clerk
Small Claims Court
Civil Court House
1 Center Street
Louisville, KS XXXXX

If your written request does not yield even a phone call to discuss the matter, you should turn up the intensity on the situation. You want to impress on the judgment debtor that you have plans to continue as a thorn in his or her life until the matter is settled. **Figure 15.2: Letter with Information on Making Payments to the Court** is designed to turn up the heat. Your first letter indicated that a copy was sent to the court, as does this letter. Although the court does not act on copies of letters, it will show the judgment debtor that you are planning your next attack.

In the letter, request that if he cannot pay the judgment all at once, he should establish a plan with the court make to payments to escrow the funds entitled to you. The letter is crafted to point out that there are methods you can use that would not be voluntary for the debtor and that the judgment debt is a matter that will affect his credit report. Although you will have to take affirmative steps to do this in some states, the lingering notion that the judgment debt could affect his or her other economic transactions may spur a movement to pay.

As long as you are communicating directly with the judgment debtor, you should suggest that he or she can always pay you and that you are ready with the necessary paperwork to wipe the judgment debt off his or her record. In the future, when you have to go through third parties, the whole level of discourse may get harsh, so keep it orderly as long as possible.

FIGURE 15.2: LETTER WITH INFORMATION ON MAKING PAYMENTS TO THE COURT

Melvin Peterson
13561 Golf Course Green
Louisville, KS XXXXX

April 10, 20XX

Mercer Martin
1441 Main Street
St. Louis, KS XXXXX

Re: Small Claims Case XXXX-XXXX-X

Dear Mr. Martin,

As you know, a judgment in the amount of $2,175.00 was entered against you in the above captioned case in Small Claims Court. If you would prefer to pay this directly to the court itself, that can be arranged by you voluntarily or by me upon motion to the court.

There is a charge for its escrow services, but it will assure you there is a record of your payment of this debt. I have sent a copy of this letter to the Chief Clerk at the

---

FIGURE 15.2: LETTER WITH INFORMATION ON MAKING PAYMENTS TO THE COURT

address below, and he is the person that you should contact to arrange this escrow payment system. As I indicated in my earlier letter, I stand ready to accept payment directly and give you an immediate Satisfaction of Judgment document to file with the court to clear your credit record.

I would appreciate your timely consideration of this debt.

Sincerely,

Melvin Peterson

Melvin Peterson

CC: Chief Clerk
Small Claims Court
Civil Court House
1 Center Street
Louisville, KS XXXXX

COLLECTION MAY BE THE MOST DIFFICULT PART

You should make a concerted effort to resolve the matter without returning to court to get its direct intervention into the collection effort. Partly, this is due to the additional fees that you may have to pay, but also it is possible that the judgment debtor has legitimate reasons he cannot pay the judgment immediately. If you fail at direct collection, you should move to get court assistance within 45 days of the judgment.

If you have collected information of the judgment debtor's assets, as outlined here, you can start with direct tactics on these assets. If you were unable to get the asset information at the time of trial, you should petition the court for a hearing to question the debtor on his or her assets or send the judgment debtor an informational subpoena — **Figure 14.1: Sample Debtor's Statement of Assets** and **Figure 14.2: Question and Answer Information Subpoena.**

If you have collected the information about the judgment debtor's asset location, you may be able to either get the court to order its use to satisfy the judgment debt or turn the matter over to the local sheriff's office as shown in **Figure 15.3: Sheriff's Income/Asset Execution Form**. The collection of your money by the sheriff will likely require an additional fee, and you may not get a reimbursement through the execution of the sheriff's recovery of your funds. Collection through a public agency will be cheaper than using a collection service later.

FIGURE 15.3: SHERIFF'S INCOME/ASSET EXECUTION FORM

City of Brentwood, Kansas — Office of Sheriff

Paul Hill

Sheriff and Marshal

Requisition for Small Claims Execution

A. Application

Plaintiff/Creditor: <u>Kensey Phillips</u>   Phone: <u>XXX-XXX-XXXX</u>   Address : <u>James Johnson</u>   Address: <u>1230 Park Avenue Street/Brentwood</u>

The Judgment was obtained in the following court:

☐Civil   ☑Small Claims

Date of Judgment: <u>2/23/20XX</u>   Amount of Judgment: <u>$568.47</u>
Court Address: <u>100 Court Circle</u>   City/Zip: <u>Brentwood, XXXXX</u>
Debtor's Name: <u>Howard Miller</u>   Address: <u>Wilson Apartments #202, Brentwood</u>
Debtor's SS#: <u>XXX-XX-XXXX</u>   Driver's Lic. #: <u>1221-1453-0876</u>

IMPORTANT — ATTACH A COPY OF YOUR COURT Judgment TO THIS APPLICATION

B. Property Execution

Debtor's Bank: <u>First National</u>   Address: <u>1401 Broad Street, Brentwood</u>
Debtor's Bank: _____ Address: _____
Debtor's Business: <u>James A1 Hardware</u> Address: <u>2190 Main Street, Brentwood</u>

FIGURE 15.3: SHERIFF'S INCOME/ASSET EXECUTION FORM

C. Income Execution

Debtor's Employer: <u>Union Iron Works, Inc.</u>
Address: <u>Malton Industrial Park, 47212 James Parkway</u> City/Zip: <u>Malton, XXXXX</u>

D. For Office Use ONLY

Interviewed by_____Mail reviewed by _____Date _____

Case #. _____Deputy_____

Dates requisitions sent to court:

1. _____ 2. _____

3. _____ 4. _____

5. _____ 6. _____

Application returned to creditor:_____

Form 109-b 6/20XX

If you have the sheriff execute an attachment of a bank account or paycheck and your judgment debt is larger than the available cash, the effect may be that the funds will continue to be taken from the bank or employer until the complete amount is satisfied. This action will depend on your state's laws. The sheriff will normally collect funds for one month before a payment is made to the judgment creditor.

As indicated above, the taking of payments out of a wage earner's paycheck is sometimes limited. Commonly, the state minimum eligibility for public assistance is used to determine the meaning of a minimum livable wage. Deductions that would leave the judgment debtor with less than this may not be allowed. You will receive only the amount above the livable wage.

In many states, the sheriff's office is too busy with criminal activity to get involved in civil matters. In these cases, you may be able to go to the court straightaway and apply for powers to seize the assets you need to satisfy your judgment directly. **Figure 15.4: Attachment of Bank Assets** shows a form the judgment creditor can fill out and submit to the clerk's office for permission to go directly to a bank where there are known assets. The bank can freeze the assets and pay them to the judgment creditor directly. Not all states allow the clerk's office this authority, but often there is a similar process through the judge who signed the original judgment.

FIGURE 15.4: ATTACHMENT OF BANK ASSETS		
Bank Execution Proceedings	STATE OF UTAH	Office of the Clerk
Application and Execution	SUPERIOR COURT	Orem, UT XXXXX
Instruction Attorney or Pro per		Assistant Clerk of the Court
1. Prepare on typewriter		1. Check the file to ensure that the information
2. Complete the application section; make original		
provided on the application is correct.		
and four copies.		2. Sign original execution.
3. Put a X in the appropriate box of the		3. Return original and two copies to applicant
"execution" section below. If box A is chosen, complete section one		4. Retain a copy in the case file.
of the Execution Claim form and attach to this form.		
4. Present original and three copies to the Clerk of the Court.		

FIGURE 15.4: ATTACHMENT OF BANK ASSETS

APPLICATION

Judgment CREDITOR: Judgment DEBTOR:

John Hallerin   Mary Martinson
1434 W. North Street   1964 N. 17th Street
Cat City, UT XXXXX   Cat City, UT XXXXX
Telephone Number: Telephone Number:
(XXX) XXX-XXXX   (XXX) XXX-XXXX

Date of Judgment: 1/29/20XX   Signed by: _John Hallerin_

Amount of Judgment: $2,451.76   Name typed: John Hallerin, Pro per

Unpaid amount of Judgment: $2,451.76   Telephone Number: XXX-XXX-XXXX

Date: 2/14/20XX:

EXECUTION

TO ANY PROPER OFFICER, whereas on said date of judgment the above named Judgment Creditor recovered judgment against the above named Judgment Debtor before the above named court for the amount of damages and costs stated above, as appears on record, whereof execution remains to be done. These are, therefore, BY AUTHORITY OF THE STATE OF UTAH TO COMMAND YOU:

☑**If the judgment debtor is a natural person:**

Within seven days from the receipt of this execution, make demand upon the main office within your county of any banking institution through any official bank officer. The above Judgment Creditor may make demand on said official for the full amount of the unpaid amount of the Judgment to be taken from any held assets with the institution of the Judgment Debtor. So long as the institution can pay the full unpaid amount of the Judgment out of said account, the banking institution may charge such service fee as the law allows for this judicial order. Should the Judgment Debtor not have sufficient assets to satisfy the judgment in full, the banking institution shall hold subsequently deposited funds and pay them out to the Judgment Creditor on a monthly basis. Any fees charged for initial and subsequent transactions shall not exceed the sum called for under Section 12-451 of the Utah Annotated Statutes.

FIGURE 15.4: ATTACHMENT OF BANK ASSETS

__ **Other:**

Within seven days from the receipt of this execution, make demand upon the main office within your county of any banking institution through any official bank officer. The above Judgment Creditor may make demand on said official for the full amount of the unpaid amount of the Judgment to be taken from any held assets with the institution of the Judgment Debtor. So long as the institution can pay the full unpaid amount of the Judgment out of said account, the banking institution may charge such service fee as the law allows for this judicial order. Said fee shall not exceed the sum called for under Section 12-451 of the Utah Annotated Statutes.

Signed (Assistant Clerk)   Date:

Laura Fernandez   4/5/20XX

The process of working through the court rarely requires you to reappear and present your case for the court to assist you in collecting. Although it is a good idea to keep copies of any letters you have written or any partial collections that have been made, the court will normally not require the documentation to intervene. If you do not have asset location information, a hearing before the court where you can question the debtor or have the court question the debtor may be the first step. First, some courts will obtain asset information through a subpoena.

Figure 15.5: Restraining Order for Bank Attachment of Assets is a typical subpoena for information where the court must be supplied information on the location of a bank asset. This can either be through the questioning of the debtor or such items as a bounced check the judgment creditor may have in his or her files from a previous payment. This orders the bank to locate, freeze, and report all assets of the judgment debtor to the court.

If assets are located, the court will have to issue a separate order to get the funds transferred either to the court's custodial account or to the creditor. In either case, it is likely that after the judgment creditor has located the assets, he or she will have to make a motion to obtain the funds frozen. You will not have to present your case again for the court's assistance.

FIGURE 15.5: RESTRAINING ORDER FOR BANK ATTACHMENT OF ASSETS

Civil Court of Hasterton County

Carson Myer
Claimant/Plaintiff

Informational Subpoena
and
Restraining Order Notice
Against

v.
Keenan Williams
Debtor/Defendant

Keenan Williams
114 Shady Lane
Rural Route 6
Coster, TN XXXXX

Jury decision in favor of Plaintiff
in the amount of $15,000 plus
cost.

THE PEOPLE OF THE STATE OF TENNESSEE

TO: Regional Branch Bank Corp. , the person to be examined and/or restrained:

A judgment has been entered on this date, in favor of the CLAIMANT and against DEBTOR in the amount of $15,000.00 , together with interest and costs and disbursements for a total of $15,000.00 , of which $15,000.00 , remains due and unpaid.

INFORMATION SUBPOENA

Because you, the person to whom this subpoena is directed either reside, are regularly employed, or have an office for the regular transaction of business in HASTERTON COUNTY of the State of Tennessee, you may answer, in writing under oath, separately and fully, each question in the questionnaire accompanying this subpoena, and you must return the answers, together with the original of the questions within, seven (7) days after your receipt of the questions and this subpoena, to Carson Myer , at Route 3, Box 733, Green Ferry Road, Coster, TN XXXXX.

FIGURE 15.5: RESTRAINING ORDER FOR BANK ATTACHMENT OF ASSETS

False swearing of failure to comply with this subpoena is punishable as a contempt of court.

RESTRAINING ORDER NOTICE

If you owe a debt to the judgment debtor or are in possession or custody of property in which the judgment debtor has an interest, be advised that in accordance with Section 323 of the state civil code, you are hereby forbidden to make or permit any sale, assignment, or transfer of, or any interference with, any such property or pay over, or otherwise dispose of any such debt except as provided in the statutes cited. This notice also covers all property which may in the future come into your possession or custody in which the judgment debtor has an interest and all debts which may come due in the future from you to the judgment debtor.

Disobedience of this Restraining Notice is punishable as a contempt of court.

_2 / 9 / 20XX_
Date

Jack Bray
Clerk of the Court

The larger the judgment debt that the settlement creates, the harder it will be to collect the full amount by one tactic. Taking a substantial part of a person's wages to satisfy a judgment is hard to tolerate for a long period of time, and if the judgment debt is large, it may take several months or years to pay in full. Unless the employee has a long record with the company that includes a good pension or other considerations such as an affordable health plan, he or she may consider finding new employment.

If the judgment creditor is lucky, the judgment debtor will simply take a second job to keep his or her family needs under control until the judgment debt is paid. The fact is that this often does not happen. The judgment debtor often changes his or her primary job, and the judgment creditor finds that payments toward the debt stop. Immediate action is necessary to again get the court to question the judgment debtor about his or her job and other assets and to start the wage attachment process anew.

More frequently than most of us imagine, the judgment debtor will move out of state to avoid the debt. This is a fact of life in our mobile society. With luck, a postal tracking as shown in **Figure 8.1: Request to Post Office for Boxholder's Address**, or a simple request for forwarding address information at the post office, will locate your judgment debtor. If the state to which the debtor has moved is near, you should have the judgment recognized in that state by filing paperwork like that in **Figure 15.6: Recognition of Out-of-State Judgment.**

FIGURE 15.6: RECOGNITION OF OUT-OF-STATE JUDGMENT	
Carson Myer Route 3, Box 733 Green Ferry Road Coster, TN XXXXX 555-515-5100 Plaintiff Pro Per	
Middlesex County Court, Civil Division Notice of Out-of-State Summary Judgment	
State of North Carolina Carson Myer	
Plaintiff	
v.	NOTICE OF MOTION
Keenan Williams	FOR SUMMARY Judgment
Defendant	
1. Take notice that the undersigned plaintiff is hereby making application to this court for a Summary Judgment in North Carolina in recognition of the Summary Judgment, hereinafter attached, which was accorded the Plaintiff by virtue of a jury trial in the State of Tennessee.	

FIGURE 15.6: RECOGNITION OF OUT-OF-STATE JUDGMENT

2. Notice of this request has been sent to the defendant by certified mail, return receipt requested, at least 30 days ahead of the filing of this Motion for Summary Judgment as required by the rules of this court. The defendant requests that the Summary Judgment of the State of North Carolina be mailed to the Plaintiff at the address above.

WHEREFORE, Plaintiff prays for speedy action so that the Judgment Debtor can be made to pay what the honorable court and its jury have awarded.

Carson Myer
_____
Carson Myer, Plaintiff in Pro Per

Although the court will provide assistance in compliance with its orders, the judgment creditor is responsible for the ultimate full collection of the debt. If you do not plan to follow through on all the necessary collection efforts, you should not start the small claims court process. Collection is more than half the battle, and, as such, this book has dedicated multiple chapters to getting the collection done. If you follow each of the suggestions contained here, your case should be one of those that is in the small percentage of cases that every dollar of the judgment debt was collected.

SUMMARY

This chapter examines the necessary paperwork you will need to start your collection process. Winning the judgment and any time spent on an appeal should make the collection effort satisfactory. You will likely have to chip away at the steps needed for easily three times as long as it took to win the dispute in your case. As you will see in the next chapter, there are ways to place attachments and liens that will assure success with time and patience.

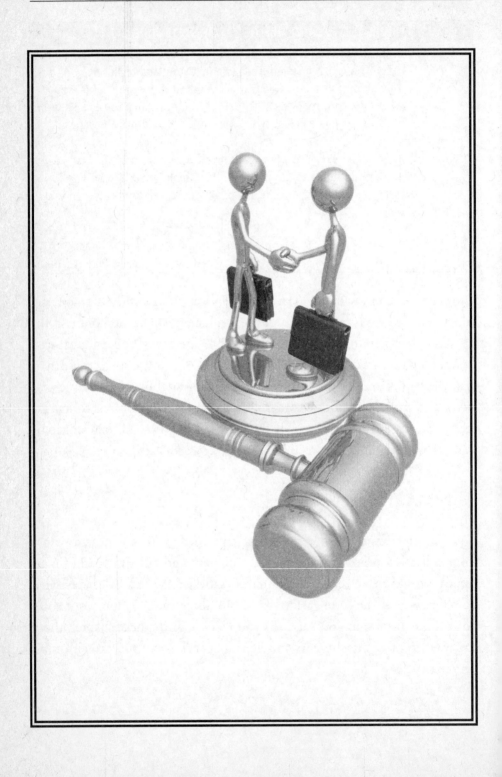

CHAPTER 16:

THE COLLECTION OF THE JUDGMENT

If your initial efforts to collect your judgment debt have not been successful, you should notify the judgment debtor that the debt is collectable for many years. Also, indicate that you will be checking for his or her employment and assets until the full amount is collected. You should immediately begin a direct search of public records for assets the debtor may own. County courthouses and state departments of vehicle registration are good places to start.

If you are getting your mail inquiries returned as undeliverable, you can ask the appeals court to modify the judgment so that the defendant will again appear in court (See **Figure 16.1: Sample Appeal to Correct Judgment Wording** for an example). If the judgment did not call for interest to be charged, this can be requested. Even if this is not approved, start trying to get the debtor back in court.

At the same time, you can make a request to have the court examine the debtor to locate his or her current assets and sources of income. This will allow you to start a new round of attachments, liens, and garnishments. You want the judgment debtor to understand that the process can be nearly endless. Because the recent changes in the bankruptcy laws have made it more difficult to nullify judgment debts, you may make significant headway in your battle.

FIGURE 16.1: SAMPLE APPEAL TO CORRECT JUDGMENT WORDING

CIVIL COURT OF THE CITY OF NEW YORK, COUNTY OF KINGS

Index No: SCC-08-12311

MACK MARTIN	
Plaintiff & Appellant	NOTICE OF
Against	SETTLEMENT
NANCY ROSS	OF TRANSCRIPT
Defendant & Respondent	

To: NANCY ROSS, DEFENDANT

Enclosed is a copy of the transcript of the above trial, along with proposed corrections, if any, which will be presented to Judge <u>Harland Parks</u> by the Appeals Clerk on <u>February 15, 20XX at 10 a.m. in the Room 422 of the courthouse</u>.

The Defendant as respondent is required to present objections, if any, to the appeals clerk at: <u>12345 Court Street, Room 1144, NY, NY XXXXX</u>.

<u>Respondent:</u>	<u>Appellant:</u>
NANCY ROSS	MACK MARTIN
1234 W. 23rd Street	1211 Park Avenue
New York, NY XXXXX	New York, NY XXXXX
Sworn before me this 28th day of January 20XX	*Mack Martin*
Sally Forthe	Appellant
Notary Public	Date: *1/28/20XX*

Use the court's subpoena power to send informational subpoenas like that shown in **Figure 14.2: Question and Answer Information Subpoena**. Because these are sent by first-class or certified mail, their cost is relatively small, and you can include a list of all financial institutions in your area for service. You will likely need to call the main office for the county or the bank's regional head office to obtain the correct name and address of the official who should be served.

The court has power in getting information. It is your responsibility to supply the request for the information and the correct service information for every subpoena. In most cases, there will be a small fee for this service. In some states, you can be given the power to collect the information directly by hand-delivering court-signed subpoenas directly to the appropriate officials. After the judgment has been issued, the court sometimes is not as particular about the service process.

If you find a financial institution with assets of the judgment debtor, you should file to take the assets through a court order similar to **Figure 16.2: Sample Court-Ordered Garnishment**. Keep records of what you get with each wage or bank garnishment so that you can ask the court for additional power to garnish wages for any remaining funds due. Finding assets through the garnishment process can continue until you are paid in full.

If you cannot locate the judgment debtor's assets yourself, you might hire an asset location service to assist you. These services will have access to such data as credit reports and other normally private records to obtain a new list of possible assets to go after. You may locate other creditors who, like yourself, are seeking to collect from the judgment debtor. Often the sharing of information can help both parties resolve their debt problems. An auto finance company may have information you are missing on the debtor's current bank account, and you might find out the debtor's current work address. You can attempt to garnish the new bank while the auto debtor goes to the debtor's work address to tow his car because of overdue payments.

You may find assets on which you can file liens or writs of attachment. Although these may not bring forth funds immediately, if the debtor ever wishes to sell or refinance the asset, your lien will have to be paid before this transaction can occur. Filing enough of such liens may ultimately deliver every penny you were owed.

COLLECTION TECHNIQUES THAT WORK

Veterans of the judgment collection wars will tell you that a varied approach works the best. After you have collected a round of what is owed to you, offer an olive branch. Once again suggest the concept of paying off the remaining debt through payments. The debtor may weigh future interruptions to his or her life from the judgment debt against an agreement he or she can make and keep over time. As soon as the debtor realizes that the presence of the judgment on his or her credit report is causing additional negative life style effects, there is most often a change in attitude.

FIGURE 16.2: SAMPLE COURT-ORDERED GARNISHMENT

CIVIL COURT OF THE CITY OF NEW YORK, COUNTY OF KINGS

Index No: SCC-08-12311

MACK MARTIN

Plaintiff

Against

NANCY ROSS

Defendant

EXECUTION
WITH NOTICE TO
GARNISHEE

The People of the State of New York

To The Sheriff or Any Marshal of The City Of New York. Greetings:

WHEREAS, in an action in the Civil Court of the City of New York, County of Kings, between __Mack Martin__, plaintiff, and who are named all the parties of the action, a judgment was entered on __January 17__, 20XX, in favor of __Mack Martin__, judgment creditor and against __Nancy Ross__, whose last known address is __108 Maple Lane, NY, NY XXXXX__ in the amount of __$17.00__ remains due and unpaid: __$974.25__ Including costs of which __$974.25__ together with interest thereon from anuary 17, 20XX__.

NOW, THEREFORE, WE COMMAND YOU to satisfy the said judgment out of the personal property of the above named judgment debtor and the debts due to him; and that the only property in which said judgment debtor who is not diseased has an interest or the debts owed to him shall be levied upon or sold hereunder; AND TO RETURN this execution to the clerk of the above captioned court within 60 days after issuance unless service of this execution is made within that time or which extensions of that time have been made by the judgment creditor or his agent.

Notice to Garnishee   To: Chemical Bank

                                      Address: 11 Wall Street, New York, NY XXXXX

FIGURE 16.2: SAMPLE COURT-ORDERED GARNISHMENT

WHEREAS, it appears that you are indebted to the judgment debtor, named above, or in possession or custody of property now capable of delivery in which the judgment debtor has an interest, including, without limitation, the following: $974.25 contained in Nancy Ross' checking account #1234567890

NOW, THEREFORE, YOU ARE REQUIRED to transfer to said sheriff or marshal, shown above, the funds of the judgment debtor that is known or believe to be within your hands.

AND TO TAKE NOTICE, that this transfer should be affected until either 90 days have passed, or the total debt has been paid to the sheriff or marshal.

AND FURTHER, TAKE NOTICE THAT the 90-day expiration may be extended by the court until the complete sum of the debt has been collected.

Dated January, 10, 20XX

Mack Martin
Mack Martin, PRO SE

The filing of the judgment debt onto the credit report is not automatic. The information from the credit agencies is uniform and established both by agreement between the credit reporting agencies and the law. To get the judgment debt on the credit record of the judgment debtor, you will need to file a form such as **Figure 16.3: File Judgment on Credit Report**. This form contains the information that Experion (Formerly TRW), Equifax, and Transunion credit reporting companies need to locate the debtor's credit records and add the new debt to the file.

These companies review the county records frequently for new information, then insert any new details into their record system. The record should appear no later than six weeks after you, as the judgment creditor, file the report with the court clerk's office. The clerk will maintain it with a copy of the actual judgment; therefore, the credit reporting company can verify the true and correct nature of the debt.

You should have done your homework on getting the court to question the debtor on such items as his or her taxpayer ID or social security number, as those will be required for this file. The law varies on the release of this information to the judgment creditor, but the court can obtain the information by a subpoena and add it to the form if necessary. You will be required to pay a fee to record this with the court clerk's office. It will remain on the judgment debtor's credit report until a Satisfaction of Judgment form is completed (explained below).

FIGURE 16.3: FILE JUDGMENT ON CREDIT REPORT

FORM UCC-1/UNIFORM COMMERCIAL CODE / FINANCING STATEMENT/ REVISED 11/20XX

PLEASE TYPE OR PRINT. CONTACT LOCAL OFFICE FOR INSTRUCTIONS.

Requesting Party: <u>Carl Cash</u> Acct #: <u>N/A</u>   SPACE FOR OFFICE USE ONLY
Address: <u>13224 Costa Viejo, Suite 4701</u>
   <u>Marvaloma, AR XXXXX</u>
   <u>(XXX) XXX-XXXX</u>

SPECIAL DEBTOR/COLLATERAL INFORMATION — CHECK AND COMPLETE IF APPLICABLE

_____a. Debtor is a transmitting utility as defined by Section 42(a) of the General Statutes of this State.

__X__b. Debtor does not have an interest of record. The name of the owner of such interest is <u>Tony Martinello</u>.

_____c. Products of collateral are claimed and covered.

_____d. The collateral is crops. Listings below described crops that are grown or will be grown on (real estate)_____.

_____e. The herein described materials are to become fixtures. Describe:

_____f. The party named in secured party block is a LESSOR, and the party named in debtor block is LESSEE.

_____g. The party named in secured party block is a CONSIGNOR, and the party named in debtor block is CONSIGNEE.

DEBTOR	Last Name	First Name	Tax ID#
	<u>Jewel</u>	<u>Mary</u>	<u>XXX-XX-XXXX</u>
Address:	<u>1487 Lillianberg Rd, Conroy, AR XXXXX</u>		
And Phone:	<u>(XXX) XXX-XXXX</u>		

FIGURE 16.3: FILE JUDGMENT ON CREDIT REPORT

SECURED	Last Name	First Name	Tax ID#
PARTY	Cash	Carl	XXX-XX-XXXX

Address: 13224 Costa Viejo, Suite 4701, Marvaloma, AR XXXXX

And Phone: (XXX) XXX-XXXX

ASSIGNEE	Last Name	First Name	Tax ID#
	Rogers Red (DBA Red's Collections)		XXX-XX-XXXX

Address: 1404 Garden St., Suite 100, Marvaloma, AR XXXXX

And Phone (XXX) XXX-XXXX

THIS FINANCING STATEMENT COVERS THE FOLLOWING ITEMS AND/OR PROPERTIES (Describe)

1487 Lillianberg Rd, Conroy, AR XXXXX

12 Martha Way, Vineyard, AR XXXXX

Ford 150 Truck, VIN 1234H87634M762, AR plate 234 MMN

Bank of Willowville, all accounts

ABC Industries, 1 Industrial Park, Williams, AR XXXXX, all wages

Number of additional sheets attached _____.

FOR CREDIT AGENCY USE:

Carl Cash

Signature of secured party

Red Rodgers

Signature of assignee

If you are the judgment debtor, there are simple ways to satisfy your obligation under the law and still make the payment of the judgment something that you can handle. You do not require much knowledge or effort to lessen the impact of losing a large judgment. One way is to write a letter to the court similar to that shown in **Figure 16.4: Letter Requesting Installment Payments**. This shows how the judgment debtor could ask the court to allow that the full payment be made in equal installments each month for two months.

If you can present adequate justification to the court about your income and assets, the judge will tailor a payment plan that satisfies the judgment debt that may not make too big of a dent in your standard of living. Hardship may not be a reason, in most states, for the forgiveness of a judgment debt, but the judge has extraordinary leeway in deciding what the payments should be and how long the debt may be stretched out.

If you need to ask the court to make arrangements for you to settle the debt over time, you should be prepared to explain the amount of your income and assets. A simple accounting of your normal income and regular itemized payments will show the judge how much discretionary spending you have available to make your judgment debt payment. You may find that the judgment creditor offers you a payment plan before you have to go to court. Try to reach an agreement first before going to the judge.

FIGURE 16.4: LETTER REQUESTING INSTALLMENT PAYMENTS

Paul Grayson
13561 Rocky Canyon Road
Telavida, GA XXXXX

May 22, 20XX

Judge Mercer Martin
Madison County Courthouse
100 West Main Street
Wyvella, GA XXXXX

Dear Judge Martin,

My name is Paul Grayson, and on January 12, 20XX, a judgment was entered against me by your court in favor of Paula White (Your Case No. 1234-567-8) for $1,200.00.

I am on a fixed income and cannot afford to pay the $1,200 all at once. I, therefore, request that the judgment be modified so I may pay her installments of $600 for two months.

I declare under penalty of perjury under the laws of the state of Georgia that the foregoing is true and correct.

> **FIGURE 16.4: LETTER REQUESTING INSTALLMENT PAYMENTS**
>
> Signed and dated August 14, 20XX.
>
> *Paul Grayson*
>
> Paul Grayson

For judgment creditors who are having trouble finding their debtor, you should not be afraid to use the local phone book. Try checking with the post office of any city where you suspect the debtor may be living. There is a small service charge — currently $1 — for looking through the records that you are seeking. If the debtor has an unusual last name, the long-distance operator for an area code can obtain information for the cost of a call to see if it is answered by your debtor or other related resident.

Reverse phone number directories found in public libraries or on the Internet can be used to locate the street address and neighbors of any debtor who has moved. A neighbor may know where he or she has moved. You can also find an up-to-date CD-ROM phone directory by calling PhoneDisc USA at 800-284-8353 or visit **www.phonedisc.com.**

IS IT BETTER TO PAY SOMEONE TO COLLECT FOR YOU?

After the judgment creditor has exhausted all the previously listed techniques, it may be worthwhile to consider the use of a professional credit bureau or agency. These normally charge 50 percent or more of the judgment debt, but you will not have to spend any additional time, effort, or cost in collecting the debt. The best kind of collection agency to use is one that is in your own town and has the local connection to continuously probe for information about the debtor and attack his or her assets and income.

A quick search of the Internet will show you that most nationwide debt collection agencies do not accept small claims court case judgment debt. It is most likely an indication that they are not effective for this task. In some states, private investigators can also collect debts, but you must be sure the contract you sign states that the agency receives a fee only if successful in making a collection.

SUMMARY

The collection process is a trauma for both the judgment debtor and judgment creditor. The judgment creditor is naturally anxious for the judgment to be paid. More often than not, this is the person who filed the first legal action. Often when a defendant wins a small claims case, there is no countersuit or cross-complaint on which to base a judgment. If the initial reason that the defendant did not offer to pay the plaintiff was a shortage of cash, payment after the judgment may be no different.

The methods listed here for collection are the best possible given the fact that some debtors will simply forever resist efforts to have the money collected. Even question- and answer-sessions before the judge on where he or she has assets and obtains income may prove to be false. Although perjury is legally punishable for debtors lying to a judge in a debtor examination session, the judge rarely suggests to the prosecutor that perjury should be pressed against the debtor. Lying under oath in some jurisdictions can be a contempt of court; however, it is also rarely enforced.

CHAPTER 17:

CLOSING OUT A CASE WHEN THE JUDGMENT HAS BEEN MET

YOU WON, BUT THERE IS STILL PAPERWORK

After the fight has ended and the judgment debtor has paid the complete amount of the award granted by the judge, there is still paperwork that needs to be completed. Until the final penny is paid, the whole judgment remains open as far as the court is concerned. Any notations on the person's credit report that were made as a result of this judgment debt remain on the records of all three national credit reporting companies.

The judgment must be cleared, and this is done by a document called a Satisfaction of Judgment, or sometimes an Acknowledgement of Satisfaction of Judgment; an example can be found in **Figure 17.1: Sample Satisfaction of Judgment**. Each court's form will be different, but the essential information is the case reference number and the names of the parties. With this information, the court clerk can find the original judgment and mark it as satisfied or paid.

The concept of satisfaction does not always mean that money has changed hands. Someone unable to pay the judgment due to a lack of assets and income might satisfy the judgment by working for the judgment creditor part time until they agree that the amount of work done is equal to the money owed in the judgment.

FIGURE 17.1: SAMPLE SATISFACTION OF JUDGMENT

Case # 171-887498-0

Judgment CREDITOR
Michael J. Miller, Pres.
Professional Services, Inc.
121 Broadway
Houston, GA XXXXX
(XXX) XXX-XXXX

JURISDICTION COURT
Superior Court of Hennpenny County
Superior Court Square, Room 101
Oakdale, GA XXXXX

RESPONDENTS
Plaintiff:
  Professional Services, Inc.
Defendant:
  Acme Janitorial

For the Use of the Court Only

ACKNOWLEDGEMENT OF SATISFACTION OF Judgment

_X_ Full   __Partial   __Matured Installment

1. Satisfaction of judgment is acknowledged as follows:
    a. _X_ Full satisfaction.
        1. _X_ The judgment was satisfied per court order.
        2. ____ The judgment creditor has accepted or performed other than the specified in the judgment in the full satisfaction of the judgment.

    b.____ The judgment has been partially satisfied. The amount paid was $____.
    c.____ The matured installments under the installment judgment have been satisfied as of this date __/__/20XX__.

2. The full name and address of the judgment creditor is: Michael J. Miller, Pres., Professional Services, Inc.,   121 Broadway, Houston, GA XXXXX

FIGURE 17.1: SAMPLE SATISFACTION OF JUDGMENT

3. Full name and address of the assignee of record is: _____

_____.

4. Full name and address of judgment debtor fully, or partially, released: <u>Acme Janitorial, 1401 14th Street, Cowin, GA XXXXX</u>

5. Judgment entered on 2/13/20XX
    Renewed on _____.

6. An <u>X</u> Abstract of Judgment _____ certified copy of the judgment is attached. The judgment was entered:

County	Date of Recording	Instrument Number
Hennpenny	6/13/20XX	14-7678-453

7. A notice of judgment lien has been filed in the Registrar of Deeds' office under file number 23-4434.

NOTICE TO THE Judgment DEBTOR: If this is an acknowledgement of full satisfaction of judgment, it will have to be recorded in each county shown in item 6 above, if any, in order to release the judgment lien and will have to be filed in the office of the Secretary of State to terminate any judgment lien on personal property.

Date: 6/13/20XX   Signed: _Michael J. Miller_

If you are the judgment debtor and the judgment creditor either refuses to sign a Satisfaction of Judgment or forgets to do so, it can be done by motion of the judgment debtor. You have the receipts showing that the debt was paid in full. Although it is the responsibility of the judgment creditor to do this, there are no-fault cases — such as a sudden death — that prevent the judgment satisfaction notice from being filed.

A letter, such as that in **Figure: 17.2: Letter Requesting Court-Ordered Satisfaction of Judgment**, can be used. The request from the judgment debtor, along with reasonable proof of the satisfaction, is normally accepted by the court. If this kind of problem occurs with the judgment debtor, he or she should also research any attachments, liens, writs, or other orders which the court has issued on the assets or income of the debtor. These ancillary documents also need to be cleared by the court.

If the original orders for the liens, writs, and attachments were issued by the court, the court can locate and release them on request of the judgment creditor. However, if the orders were placed through a different government agency, such as the sheriff's office or the recorder of deeds, the judgment debtor must locate them and present them to the court clerk. A record may not exist in the small claims court clerk's office without this additional effort. The judgment creditor needs to be diligent in releasing all these marks on the debtor's record.

FIGURE 17.2: LETTER REQUESTING COURT-ORDERED SATISFACTION OF JUDGMENT

Paul Grayson
13561 Rocky Canyon Road
Telavida, GA XXXXX

Judge Mercer Martin   May 22, 20XX
Madison County Courthouse
100 West Main Street
Wyvella, GA XXXXX

Dear Judge Martin,

My name is Paul Grayson, and on January 12, 20XX, a judgment was entered against me by your court in favor of Paula White (Your Case No. 1234-567-8) for $1,200.00.

I paid Mrs. White by personal check (certified bank copy attached) [OR I paid her installments of $600 for 2 months. My certified bank copies of these checks are attached.] She, however, has refused to provide an Acknowledgement of Satisfaction of Judgment.

My last correspondence to her has come back, addressee moved, left no forwarding address. I now have no way of getting this judgment off my record.

Could you arrange for the judgment to show it has been satisfied?

> **FIGURE 17.2: LETTER REQUESTING COURT-ORDERED SATISFACTION OF JUDGMENT**
>
> I declare under penalty of perjury under the laws of the state of Georgia that the foregoing is true and correct.
>
> Signed and dated August 14, 20XX.
>
> *Paul Grayson*
> _____
> Paul Grayson

If the original process by which the various freeze mechanisms were placed turn out to be a complex one, it is possible that only the judgment creditor knows all that he or she did to try to collect the monies owed. Notwithstanding the complexity of the job, it is the judgment creditor that should have the records necessary to change all that he did to assure that no assets were relinquished by the debtor until the judgment was fully satisfied.

It is also required of the judgment creditor to reverse these collection acts. If the person refuses to do so, the court may not consider authorizing the next garnishment when the judgment creditor appears in court. Creditors must remember that they are dealing with justice at the county level — in most cases — and there are core officials that make their administrative jobs their careers. If you make more work for them, you may not get help in the future.

The small claims court system can be useful. Some kinds of businesses will find it particularly appealing for taking care of bounced checks and other debt problems. The system cannot work if people let their grudges continue after the court has righted the injustice. Cases where judgment creditors make a pattern of failing to file closing paperwork will be known by the judge who makes future decisions on his cases.

SUMMARY

This chapter was the final step in the legal process. After the case has been built, tried, and a judgment issued, then the debt must be paid so it can be properly closed. This chapter provided the legal information necessary for either party to release any pending legal attachments, liens, wage garnishments, or writs. The judgment debtor should also provide the credit bureau with information as to the date, time, and method of the debt discharge, just in case it was not picked up in the bureau's review of the court's recent records.

APPENDIX: A

GLOSSARY OF LEGAL TERMS

Abstract of judgment: A document issued by the clerk of the court after the trial has ended that summarizes the decision of the judge.

Abuse of process: An improper or malicious use of the criminal process.

Accord and satisfaction: A compromise of both parties on the amount of money or other valuable considerations that will be accepted as the settlement of a case.

Acknowledgement of satisfaction of judgment: A form that is executed and recorded with the court when a judgment against one party has been paid to the other party.

Action of law: A judicial proceeding where one party prosecutes another party for a wrong done.

Actionable: A deed or other action that gives rise to a judgment action in the court.

Actual damages: Those damages or costs that are directly related to the specific breach or tort that the court finds were sustained and caused by the plaintiff.

Adjournment: Ordered by a judge to temporarily end court action at a given time with a set date to resume at another time or place.

Adjudicate: When a judge is called on to render a legally binding decision.

Adjudication: The judge's decision on a specific case.

Admissible evidence: Evidence that is properly and legally used in presentation of a case before a judge or magistrate.

Admission: A written or oral statement sworn under penalty of perjury claiming certain facts to be true.

Adversary system: A type of dispute resolution that uses a trial before a judge or a jury that is practiced in the United States.

Adverse witness: A witness who is testifying for the other side of the case.

Affidavit: A sworn statement made before a notary public or judge.

Affirm: To make a solemn statement before the court.

Affirmative defense: A defense in which the facts of the case are admitted, but a justification is not considered the defendant's responsibility.

Allegation: A statement, either written or oral, with the facts of a case that has not yet been proved.

Allege: To say that a fact is true before it is proven.

Alternative dispute resolution (ADR): Method of resolving a dispute without going to trial, such as mediation or arbitration.

Amend: A statement or document introduced to change the claim currently on file.

American Arbitration Association (AAA): A national organization designed to provide qualified arbitrators with special knowledge suitable to the facts of a case, often used in civil and labor disputes.

Answer: A written statement of the defendant's case in which the plaintiff's claims are admitted or denied. A written answer is not required in a small claims case. The defendant notifies the court and the plaintiff that he wants to contest the plaintiff's claim by filing the appearance.

Appeal: A process for requesting a formal change of decision, typically to a higher court.

Appearance: The paper the defendant in a small claims case files and also sends to the plaintiff to notify them that the defendant wants to participate in the case.

Appellant: The party in a case who appeals the case to a higher court.

Appellate court: The specific court that the law says has the power to review a particular lower court's decision.

Appellee: A person who answers an appeal to a higher court.

Application for waiver of court fees and costs: This is an application that permits the filing of a case or counterclaim without paying fees, due to a verified hardship the paying of the fees would cause.

Arbitration: A dispute is turned over to an arbitrator, who is impartial to both parties in the case. The decision is normally binding on both parties and may not be retried or appealed.

Arbitration clause: A clause often inserted in contracts or warranty documents that requires the case to be settled by an arbitrator, not a court.

Arbitrator: A private, disinterested person agreed to by both parties who will review the presentations of both sides and make a binding decision on the case.

Asset: The entirety of a person, corporation, or organization's real and personal property.

Assignee: A person, often from a collection agency, who stands before a court representing the prevailing party in a case.

Attachment: The act of taking, appending to the title, or seizing a person's personal property by a writ issued by the court.

Attachment execution: A document that attaches or garnishes the assets of a person to pay the judgment of the court. It is not used in all states.

Bad faith: When a person willfully fails to comply with his or her statutory responsibility or contractual obligations.

Bank levy: A court-ordered document that forces a bank, credit union, savings and loan association, or other financial institution to pay the defendant's financial assets to the plaintiff.

Breach of contract: A failure, without legal cause or justification, to perform all or part of a contract that has been made between the defendant and the plaintiff.

Burden of proof: The duty of a party to substantiate an allegation or issue to convince the court as to the truth of the claim.

Calendar: The day's schedule of court cases to be heard in a given courtroom.

Capacity: This is the legal term for judging a plaintiff's or defendant's ability to understand the nature and effects of their actions on the issues of the legal matter before the court.

Caption: The title at the top of all papers in a court case.

Cause of action: The factual basis of the case.

Chambers: The judge's personal office.

Civil action: All legal matters that are not criminal in nature.

Civil court: The court that handles disputes that are resolved arising out of common law and civil statutes. It does not handle criminal cases.

Civil law: This is the body of law that applies to all noncriminal actions.

Circumstantial evidence: Evidence not based on witness observation or actual physical presentation of evidence.

Claim of exemption: A document the debtor files with the court claiming certain property to be exempt from use as payments due as a result of these cases. In some states, cars needed to drive to work and homesteaded homes are examples of these types of properties.

Claim splitting: The prohibited practice of dividing the case into two or more actions to receive more than the monetary limit imposed on small claims court matters in a state. The practice puts the defendant in double jeopardy.

Clean hands doctrine: This doctrine means that the plaintiff must not be guilty of any wrongdoing in connection with his or her case.

Collateral: Most often, property that is pledged for additional security for the repayment of a debt or loan.

Complaint: The paper the plaintiff files outlining the claim against the defendant.

Confession of judgment: This is an admission of a debt by the debtor, which may be entered into the records of the court as a judgment, without needing to provide formal proof of its existence.

Consequential damages: Any damages that were caused by an injury but are not necessarily the direct result of the injury. Loss of work due to an injury, for example, may be considered a consequential damage in some states. The court requires that each consequential damage have its own separate proof.

Costs: These are the fees and costs associated with the case that the prevailing party had to pay to bring the suit to court.

Counterclaim: A claim filed by a defendant against the plaintiff following the filing of the original claim of the plaintiff against the defendant.

Court: A branch of government responsible for resolving disputes arising under law. Small claims court may be a division of the normal civil court system or part of a system administrated by a magistrate.

Creditor: The person to whom a debtor owes money.

Cross-claim: A complaint filed against the plaintiff of the original action by the original defendant. These cases are often joined and heard at the same time as one case.

Cross-examination: The testimony from a witness who has been called on and questioned by the opposition in a case. You have a right to cross-examine witnesses of the opposition.

Damages: The monetary compensation the court awards to the injured party to compensate for his or her loss in an injury, breach of contract, or tort case.

DBA: An acronym for "Doing Business As."

Debt: The sum of money due as a result of the judgment or an agreement between the parties.

Debtor: The person who owes the debt.

Default: When a properly served party to a lawsuit fails to appear at the small claims court on the date and time required.

Default judgment: This goes into effect when the defendant fails to respond or show up to defend against the statement of claim. The clerk or judge may enter a default judgment against that person.

Defendant: In a civil case, the person(s) or corporation against whom the plaintiff has filed the claim. If an individual is being sued, he or she must be at least 18 years old.

Defense: Conducted in court by witnesses, evidence, or arguments in opposition to the material presented by the opposing party.

Demand for arbitration: When a filing for mandated arbitration of a contract requiring arbitration as the method of dispute settlement happens, the demand for arbitration is used.

Deposition: A written, video, or oral questioning before an independent third party, such as a court reporter.

Discovery: The gathering of evidence before the case goes to trial through the use of depositions, requests for admissions, or interrogatories.

Dismiss with prejudice: To set aside the suit representing the dispute and denying the right to reopen, retrial, or re-file the dispute as another case in the future.

Dismiss without prejudice: The court sets aside the suit representing the dispute and grants the right to reopen, retrial, or re-file the dispute as another case.

Docket: The court's record of the chronological history of the case.

Enforce: To place the judgment into effect by taking separate necessary legal steps to force compliance with the court's decision.

Evidence: Any form of proof presented by a party for the purpose of supporting its arguments before the court. This includes witness testimony and papers, photographs, or other entities related to the issues.

Execution of judgment: The method by which the person winning the suit, also known as the prevailing party, collects the money, property, or action ordered in the judgment.

Exempt assets: Properties that are protected from being used to settle a dispute by the force of an existing law. For example, some states will exempt a certain portion of wages necessary for sustenance from a garnishment.

Filing fees and court costs: The costs that a plaintiff must pay to file a small claims action or suit, which are paid to the clerk of court. These costs may be recovered from the defendant if the suit has been resolved in the plaintiff's favor.

Fraud: A false representation of a fact through the use of words, conduct, misleading allegation, or concealment. This representation is fraud if it deceives or is intended to deceive another person and causes an injury to that person.

Fraudulent conveyance: The transference of the title to real or personal property with the intent of delaying or defrauding creditors.

Garnish: When the wages or property of the debtor in a lawsuit are attached.

Garnishment: The legal process available to collect a debt from the debtor's wages or other cash assets. Garnishment processes vary from state to state. They may be exercised through part of the small claims court process or a separate enforcement agency on receiving a copy of the judgment.

General damages: Those damages that are directly caused by actions covered in a contract. Damages that are due to a failure to follow the contract are deemed the result of a tort. General damages can be proven readily through the presentation of evidence. These damages are due the injured party as a matter of law.

Good cause: A legally sufficient reason.

Grace period: The time granted for payment without penalty; found in a contract.

Grantor: A company or insurer that has agreed to be responsible for the acts or omissions of another.

Guaranty: An agreement is made by a party to be responsible for the performance or payments of another if that person reneges on the promise in the underlying agreement.

Guardian ad litem: A person appointed by the courts to represent a minor or a person incapable of making his or her own decisions. In the case of a minor, this guardian replaces the parents for all legal decisions.

Hearsay: Evidence based on what a witness has heard someone else say, rather than what the witness has experienced.

Homestead exemption: In some states, the head of a household may designate a house and a certain amount of land as his or her homestead. This homestead is exempt from general debt collection. Often, the exception is any mortgage on the homesteaded property itself.

Impound: When real or personal property is put in the custody of a third party.

In rem: The debt is against a property instead of the person who may own the property.

Inadmissible: Information or testimony that, under the established rules of evidence, cannot be admitted or received in court.

Indemnification clause: This type of contract clause says that one party will indemnify the other party against damages in connection with the performance of the contract.

Indemnify: To hold a party harmless for a damage or loss that occurred in the past or that may occur in the future.

Injunction: A judicial order requiring either party in a case to perform a specific action or remedy as called for in the order.

Injury: Any damage done to another person's body, reputation, or property.

Judge: The individual who presides in a particular session of a court. The function of a judge is to use the rule of law to determine the fairest resolution to disputes.

Judgment: The judge's written ruling on the case.

Judgment creditor: The person in a case who has won the judgment and is owed an amount of funds from the debtor.

Judgment debtor: The person who has lost the decision of the court and owes a debt to the other party of the action.

Judgment debtor's statement of assets: A form often used by judges to obtain a list of the debtor's assets and sources of income.

Judgment execution: The formal written document that is registered with the court clerk showing which assets and financial resources are to be seized and used to satisfy the judgment of the case.

Judgment-proof: Attorneys and bill collectors use this term to refer to a litigant who is unlikely to pay a debt ordered by the court due to an extreme lack of assets from which anyone can legally attach any wealth. A judgment-proof litigant is a bad choice as a target of a small claims court suit. You may win easily but never collect any money.

Legal capacity: This term refers to individuals who do not meet certain minimum standards to have the capacity to be sued. Included in this group are persons not of sound mind, persons under the legal age of responsibility, and persons of legal disabilities.

Levy: In some circumstances, this is used to seize property to satisfy a judgment.

Liability: A person's obligation to do, or refrain from doing, a particular act. The court may establish a debt from one party to the other party, and this debt is considered a liability to be paid.

Lien: A legally registered claim against the property of another person who represents a security that the debt will be paid.

Lis pendens: See mechanic's lien.

Litigant: The plaintiff or defendant in a suit.

Malicious abuse of legal process: This occurs when someone willfully misapplies the powers of the court in a manner not intended by the court itself.

Mechanic's lien: This type of lien is placed on real or personal property, preventing its sale or transfer until the complete debt amount of the lien has been paid. Real property with either a mechanic's lien or a lis pendens attached may not be sold or have other loans released or refinanced before this lien has been cleared through payment of the debt.

Mediation: A voluntary way to avoid a full trial. A mediator is an independent individual, sometimes paid for or required by the court, who meets with both parties in an attempt to find a settlement or compromise that avoids the necessity of a formal trial.

Mediator: The independent person who tries to assist in the settlement of a dispute between two parties. See mediation.

Motion: A request that a party makes to the court, asking the court to take some type of action. For example, a motion for a continuance requests the court to postpone a court hearing or a trial. A motion for reconsideration asks the court to review and reconsider the court's decision.

Net income: This term varies from state to state. It is defined as the gross income of an individual, less withholding of taxes, social security, or legal deductions (such as health insurance). It may also be reduced in some states by exemption for such things as a minimum living wage or living allowance.

Net worth: The assets of an individual less any outstanding debts.

Nominal damages: A trivial sum that is awarded to indicate fault in an action and the fact that damages were caused.

Notary public: A person recognized by the state as an individual who can witness and certify the validity of a person's signature.

Notation of appeal: Notice of appeal to a higher court or for a rehearing in small claims court, whichever is allowed in your state.

Notice of entry of judgment: The formal statement to both parties in a case giving the judge's decision or judgment.

Notice of motion to vacate judgment: A request by one of the parties of the action that the judgment be set aside and a new hearing be set.

Objection: A formal protest made by a party over the testimony or evidence that the other side is trying to introduce.

Order to appear for examination: This is a collection hearing where the debtor is ordered to appear before the court to present his or her property and sources of income. In some states, this examination is requested by the injured party, and the party is allowed to assist the judge in asking specific questions.

Per say: See pro se.

Perjury: Any false statement made on purpose under oath in a courtroom.

Personal jurisdiction: The power of the court over an individual defendant.

Personal service: Handing a copy of a court document directly to the person to be served.

Petitioner: One who presents (files) a petition to a court against a respondent. This is similar to a plaintiff in a criminal or civil case.

Plaintiff: The person filing the case requesting that the court require the defendant to either pay a certain amount or perform some act. The plaintiff must be at least 18 years old. If under 18, the plaintiff must have an adult file the case on his or her behalf.

Pleadings: Requests that either the plaintiff or defendant makes to the judge during the trial.

Pretrial conference: A court hearing for the judge to review the case before the trial date.

Pro se: A Latin phrase meaning "for himself; in his own behalf; in person" or as in appearing for oneself. This is to act as one's own attorney in a civil or criminal matter.

Pro tem judge: A lawyer with at least five years of experience in case law and appointed to serve as a temporary judge to relieve the load of regular judges.

Process: Court papers that are used to notify a person, business, corporation, or limited liability company that he, she, or it is being sued.

Process server: An independent person or a person not legally related to the case or parties of a case who delivers the process of the court to one or another party to the suit.

Proof of service: A form signed by the person serving a party or witness to a lawsuit.

Reformation: An equitable settlement that includes, at least in part, the rewriting of a contract to remedy an inequity or mistake.

Release: A form signed by one party releasing another party from an obligation he or she has to the original party.

Relief: What the plaintiff requests the defendant exercise to resolve the suit. This may involve performing an act that ends the dispute.

Repudiation: A declaration by one of the parties of a contract suggesting that he or she is not willing to perform all or part of a contract.

Request for dismissal: A form to notify the small claims court that a settlement has been reached by the parties before the trial.

Request to correct or vacate a judgment: This is a motion filed with the court on a form to request the cancellation of the judgment.

Request to pay judgment in installments: A form filed with the court requesting approval for the judgment to be paid over time, undersigned by both parties and including terms such as the interest charged, monthly payment amount due, and terms if there is a default.

Request to pay judgment to the court: This is a request by either party in the case for the judgment to be paid to the court and then dispersed to the winning party.

Rescission: A cancellation of a contract by the court to put both parties in the positions they were in before the contract was signed.

Respondent: The person who answers various legal proceedings. This is similar to a defendant in a criminal or civil case.

Response: See answer.

Restitution: The act of giving back an equal amount of value to compensate for costs, injuries, or losses.

Return date: The date by which the defendant must file his or her appearance to formally notify the court he or she wishes to contest the plaintiff's complaint. If the defendant does not file an appearance or attend the return date, a default judgment may be entered against him or her.

Satisfaction of judgment: This confirms that the terms in the judgment have been met by the defendant and the issue is resolved.

Service by publication: This method is used to notify the small claims court that a settlement has been reached by the parties before the trial.

Service of process: When the plaintiff gives the defendant adequate notice of being sued. The defendant is given a copy of the statement of claim.

Small claims action: A legal case filed in the county court that requests damages in the form of money or property with a value of $5,000 or less or asks the defendant to perform some act that solves the problem.

Statement of claim: The written pleading or form that says the parties' names, the facts, circumstances, and nature of the case; the amount or value of the dispute; and the resolution or outcome requested by the plaintiff.

Statute of limitations: The time the law says you have to bring certain kinds of disputes before the court.

Stay: An order by the judge delaying or suspending some action of the proceeding until a specific future date stipulated.

Stipulation or mediated agreement: The result of a process in which the plaintiff and defendant reach a written resolution to the dispute, either by themselves or with the help of a neutral mediator.

Subpoena: A document issued by the court to compel a witness to appear and give testimony or to procure documentary evidence in a proceeding.

Subpoena duces tecum: A court order requiring a party to produce a certain document to the court by a specified time.

Substitute service: Serving the sued party by leaving the court papers with someone else. This may imply that the company is served through an employee rather than its owner or corporate president.

Summons: The paper the clerk of court issues that is used to notify the defendant that the plaintiff has filed a lawsuit against him. The summons must be served on the defendant properly. In a small claims case, it must tell the defendant the date and time of the return date.

Tangible property: Real or personal property that is capable of being possessed.

Tax: The sum of money assessed on real property, personal or corporate income, or, in some cases, personal property.

Tenancy at will: The right to occupy a property at will and for an indefinite period of time.

Testimony: The sworn evidence presented by witnesses.

Tort: A civil or private wrong.

Trial: The court proceeding in which the plaintiff and defendant present evidence to the judge for ruling on the case.

Trial date: The date set by the court for the case trial.

Usurious contract: A contract that contains interest charges that, if imposed, would violate the highest rate allowed by state law.

Venue: The venue is the county in which the case should be filed.

Wage garnishment: A legal action that requires the debtor's employer to withhold a portion of the debtor's wages to pay a judgment issued by the court.

Waive: When a person abandons or gives up the right to a certain legal protection.

Writ of execution: A document that directs the sheriff or other legal authority to enforce the order or judgment of the court.

RESOURCES BY STATE

INFORMATION COMPILED JULY 2009

ALABAMA

Monetary limit: $3,000

General statute of limitations: Written contracts, six years; oral contracts, six years; personal injury, two years; and property damage, six years.

Time limit the judgment is valid: 20 years

Time limit for debtor to pay (or set up payment schedule): 14 days

State-mandated costs and fees: $125 maximum*

Small claims court Web site: www.judicial.state.al.us

Information Web sites:
www.consumeraffairs.com/consumerism/small_al.html

Debt collection law: Alabama Code Section 40-12-80 et seq.

Location within state of the Federal Small Claims Tax Court:
Birmingham, Mobile

Where to sue: The county where an individual defendant resides has venue. The county where a company or corporation has a business office.

*Fees vary from county to county, but this is the state-mandated minimum fee.

ALASKA

Monetary limit: $10,000

General statute of limitations: Written contracts, three years; oral contracts, three years; personal injury, two years; and property damage, three years.

Time limit the judgment is valid: 10 years

Time limit for debtor to pay (or set up payment schedule): To be agreed upon between the creditor and debtor

State-mandated costs and fees: $75 maximum

Small claims court Web site: www.state.ak.us/courts/forms.htm#sc

Information Web sites: www.state.ak.us/courts/forms/sc-100.pdf
http://law.freeadvice.com/resources/smallclaimscourts.htm
www.consumeraffairs.com/consumerism/small_ak.html
touchngo.com/lglcntr/akstats/Statutes/Title22/Chapter15/
Section040.htm

Debt collection law: Alaska Statutes Section 8.24.0.011 et seq.

Location within state of the Federal Small Claims Tax Court: Anchorage

Where to sue: The county where an individual defendant resides or is employed has venue. The county where a company or corporation has a business office.

ARIZONA

Monetary limit: $2,500

General statute of limitations: Written contracts, six years; oral contracts, three years; personal injury, two years; and property damage and money debts, three years.

Time limit the judgment is valid: 6 years maximum

Time limit for debtor to pay (or set up payment schedule): Immediately or creditor can establish wage garnishment

State-mandated costs and fees: $16

Small claims court Web site: www.supreme.state.az.us/Info/brochures/smclaims.htm

Information Web sites: www.supreme.state.az.us/Info/brochures/smclaims.htm
www.consumeraffairs.com/consumerism/small_az.html
research.Lawyers.com/Arizona/Arizona-Small-Claims.html

Debt collection law: Arizona Revised Statutes Annotated Section 32-1001 et seq.

Location within state of the Federal Small Claims Tax Court: Phoenix

Where to sue: The county where an individual defendant resides has venue or transaction/injury occurred. The county where a company or corporation has a business office.

ARKANSAS

Monetary limit: $5,000

General statute of limitations: Written contracts, five years; oral contracts and money damages, three years; personal injury, three years; and property damage, three years.

Time limit the judgment is valid: 10 years (5 years if Justice of Pease Court)

Time limit for debtor to pay (or set up payment schedule): 10 days.

State-mandated costs and fees: $25* minimum

Small claims court Web site: http://courts.state.ar.us/documents/small_claims_info.pdf

Information Web sites: www.arkbar.com/publications/pdf/scc_toc.pdf www.consumeraffairs.com/consumerism/small_ar.html www.districtcourtfortsmith.org/Civil%20Small%20Claims.htm

Debt collection law: Arkansas Statutes Annotated Section 617-21-104 et seq.

Location within state of the Federal Small Claims Tax Court: Little Rock

Where to sue: The county where an individual defendant resides has venue. The county where a company or corporation has a business office.

*This is the state-mandated fee at the time of writing this book. Counties can add charges as set by the county government.

CALIFORNIA

Monetary limit: $7,500; Plantiff cannot file claim over $2,500 more than twice a year; $5,000 business limit.

General statute of limitations: Written contracts, four years; oral contracts and car accidents, two years; personal injury, two years; and property damage and money owed, three years.

Time limit the judgment is valid: 10 years

Time limit for debtor to pay (or set up payment schedule): 10 days after 30-day appeal period

State-mandated costs and fees: $75* maximum

Small claims court Web site: www.courtinfo.ca.gov/selfhelp/smallclaims

**Information Web sites: http://research.Lawyers.com/California/California-Small-Claims.html
www.smallclaimshelpline.com
www.kinseyLaw.com/freestuff/selfhelp/smallclaims/freesmallclaim forms.html**

Debt collection law: California Civil Code Section 1788 et seq.

Location within state of the Federal Small Claims Tax Court: Fresno, Los Angeles, San Diego, San Francisco

Where to sue: The county where an individual defendant resides (or resided at time that obligation was created) has venue. The county where a company or corporation has a business office.

*Fees within the state vary, as they are set by the state, county, and county sheriff. Study the fee schedule carefully, as there is a different fee for each case monetary size and also all special services required beyond the filing of the complaint with the local court.

COLORADO

Monetary limit: $7,500

General statute of limitations: Written contracts, six years; oral contracts or recovery of money, six years; personal injury, two years; and property damage, two years.

Time limit the judgment is valid: 20 years

Time limit for debtor to pay (or set up payment schedule): 10 days

State-mandated costs and fees: $23* maximum

Small claims court Web site: www.courts.state.co.us/Forms/Forms_List.cfm/Form_Type_ID/9

Information Web sites: www.consumeraffairs.com/consumerism/small_co.html
http://research.Lawyers.com/Colorado/Colorado-Small-Claims.html
public.findLaw.com/litigation_appeals/colorado-small-claims.html

Debt collection law: Colorado Revised Statues Section 5-10101 et seq. and 12-14-101 et seq.

Location within state of the Federal Small Claims Tax Court: Denver

Where to sue: The county where an individual defendant resides, attends school, or is employed has venue. The county where a company or corporation has a business office.

*This is for filing the claim only and depends on the amount of the suit. There are many other fees possible if court service or documents are needed.

CONNECTICUT

Monetary limit: $5,000 excluding security deposit claims

General statute of limitations: Written contracts, six years; oral contracts, three years; personal injury, three years; and property damage, three years.

Time limit the judgment is valid: 20-25 years

Time limit for debtor to pay (or set up payment schedule): 30 days

State-mandated costs and fees: $35

Small claims court Web site: www.jud.ct.gov/directory/directory/directions/smallclaims.htm

Information Web sites: www.research.Lawyers.com/Connecticut/Connecticut-Small-Claims.html
www.consumeraffairs.com/consumerism/small_ct.html
www.infoline.org/informationlibrary/Documents/Small%20Claims.asp

Debt collection law: Connecticut General Statutes Annotated Section 36-243 et seq.; 42-127 et seq.

Location within state of the Federal Small Claims Tax Court: Hartford

Where to sue: The county where an individual defendant resides has venue or where the transaction occurred. The county where a company or corporation has a business office.

DELAWARE

Monetary limit: $15,000

General statute of limitations: Written contracts, three years; oral contracts, three years; personal injury, three years; and property damage, two years.

Time limit the judgment is valid: 3 years

Time limit for debtor to pay (or set up payment schedule): Must be agreed upon outside of court

State-mandated costs and fees: $50 maximum

Small claims court Web site: http://courts.delaware.gov/How%20To/ court%20proceedings/?JPCourt.htm

Information Web sites: www.consumeraffairs.com/consumerism/ small_de.html
research.lawyers.com/Delaware/Delaware-Small-Claims.html
law.freeadvice.com/resources/smallclaimscourts.htm

Debt collection law: Delaware Code Annotated Title 30, Section 2301(13)

Location within state of the Federal Small Claims Tax Court: None

Where to sue: The county where an individual defendant resides has venue. The county where a company or corporation has a business office.

DISTRICT OF COLUMBIA

Monetary limit: $5,000

General statute of limitations: Written contracts, three years; oral contracts, three years; personal injury, three years; and property damage, three years.

Time limit the judgment is valid: 20 years

Time limit for debtor to pay (or set up payment schedule): 10 days

District Mandated Costs and Fees: $45

Small claims court Web site: www.dccourts.gov/dccourts/superior/ civil/small_claims.jsp

Information Web sites: www.consumeraffairs.com/consumerism/ small_dc.html ann.sagepub.com/cgi/reprint/287/1/21?ck=nck law.freeadvice.com/resources/smallclaimscourts.htm

Debt collection law: Federal Code Annotated Section 22-3423 et seq.; 28-3814 et seq.

Location within state of the Federal Small Claims Tax Court: Washington

Where to sue: The district has venue only if individual defendant resides or company has a business office in the district.

FLORIDA

Monetary limit: $5,000

General statute of limitations: Written contracts, five years; oral contracts, four years; personal injury, four years; and property damage, four years.

Time limit the judgment is valid: 20 years

Time limit for debtor to pay (or set up payment schedule): 14 days

State-mandated costs and fees: 300 maximum

Small claims court Web site: www.circuit8.org/sc

Information Web sites: www.consumeraffairs.com/consumerism/ small_fl.html http://public.findlaw.com/litigation_appeals/florida-small-claims.html http://research.lawyers.com/Florida/Florida-Small-Claims.html

Debt collection law: Florida Statutes Section 559.55 et. seq.

Location within state of the Federal Small Claims Tax Court:
Jacksonville, Miami, Tallahassee, Tampa

Where to sue: The county where an individual defendant resides has
venue. The county where a company or corporation has a business office.

*Florida filing fees vary from county to county. The only accurate way to
estimate these fees and costs is to contact the court clerk in the county in
which you plan to file your suit.

GEORGIA

Monetary limit: $15,000 (No limit in eviction cases)

General statute of limitations: Written contracts, six years; oral contracts,
four years; personal injury, two years; and property damage, four years.

Time limit the judgment is valid: 7 years

Time limit for debtor to pay (or set up payment schedule): 30 days

State-mandated costs and fees: $50* maximum

**Small Claims (or Magistrate) Court Web site: http://consumer.georgia.
gov/00/article/0,2086,5426814_39039081_39334516,00.html**

**Information Web sites: www.consumeraffairs.com/consumerism/
small_ga.html
http://law.freeadvice.com/resources/smallclaimscourts.htm
http://research.lawyers.com/Georgia/Georgia-Small-Claims.html**

Debt collection law: Georgia Code Annotated Section 7-3-1 et seq.

Location within state of the Federal Small Claims Tax Court: Atlanta

Where to sue: The county where an individual defendant resides has venue. The county where a company or corporation has a business office.

*Some counties have extra or additional fees.

HAWAII

Monetary limit: $3,500

General statute of limitations: Written contracts, six years; oral contracts, six years; personal injury, two years; and property damage, two years.

Time limit the judgment is valid: 10 years

Time limit for debtor to pay (or set up payment schedule): 30 days

State-mandated costs and fees: $35* minimum

Small claims court Web site: http://www.courts.state.hi.us/page_server/SelfHelp/SmallClaims/695F88B9A961B33EAB295F3B7.html

Information Web sites: www.consumeraffairs.com/consumerism/small_hi.html
http://research.lawyers.com/Hawaii/Hawaii-Small-Claims.html
http://en.wikipedia.org/wiki/Hawaii_State_Small_Claims_Court

Debt collection law: Hawaii Revised Statues Section 443-B-1 et seq.

Location within state of the Federal Small Claims Tax Court: Honolulu

Where to sue: The judicial district where an individual defendant resides has venue. The county where a company or corporation has a business office.

*There is a complicated array of fees for this court. Ask the court clerk to estimate costs based on the type of case, the services, and documents you will need.

IDAHO

Monetary limit: $5,000

General statute of limitations: Written contracts, five years; oral contracts, four years; personal injury, two years; and property damage, 36 years.

Time limit the judgment is valid: 5 years

Time limit for debtor to pay (or set up payment schedule): 14 days

State-mandated costs and fees: $30

Small claims court Web site: www.isc.idaho.gov/material.htm*

Information Web sites: www.consumeraffairs.com/consumerism/small_id.html
http://research.lawyers.com/Idaho/Idaho-Small-Claims.html

Debt collection law: Idaho Code Section 26-222 et seq.

Location within state of the Federal Small Claims Tax Court: Boise, Pocatello

Where to sue: The county where an individual defendant resides has venue. The county where a company or corporation has a business office.

*This site has many useful documents and videos in both English and Spanish.

ILLINOIS

Monetary limit: $10,000 (No limit on evictions)

General statute of limitations: Written contracts, one year; oral contracts, five years; personal injury, two years; and property damage, five years.

Time limit the judgment is valid: 20 years

Time limit for debtor to pay (or set up payment schedule): 30 days

State-mandated costs and fees: $105-$190

Small claims court Web site: www.ag.state.il.us/consumers/smlclaims.html

Information Web sites: www.19thcircuitcourt.state.il.us/self-help/s_claims/index.htm
www.consumeraffairs.com/consumerism/small_il.html
www.law.siu.edu/selfhelp/info/court/smallclaims.pdf

Debt collection law: Illinois Annotated Statutes. Chapter 111 Section 201 et seq.

Location within state of the Federal Small Claims Tax Court: Chicago, Peoria

Where to sue: The county where an individual defendant resides has venue. The county where a company or corporation has a business office.

INDIANA

Monetary limit: $6,000

General statute of limitations: Written contracts, six years; oral contracts, six years; personal injury, two years; and property damage, two years.

Time limit the judgment is valid: 10 years

Time limit for debtor to pay (or set up payment schedule): No limit, depends on creditor's diligence to collect and debtor's ability to pay

State-mandated costs and fees: $70

Small claims court Web site: http://www.in.gov/judiciary/rules/ small_claims/

Information Web sites: www.research.lawyers.com/Indiana/Indiana- Small-Claims.html
www.consumeraffairs.com/consumerism/small_in.html
www.indy.gov/eGov/Courts/Pages/smallclaims.aspx

Debt collection law: Indiana Statutes Annotated, Title 33, Article 28, Chapter 3, Sections 1-10.

Location within state of the Federal Small Claims Tax Court: Indianapolis

Where to sue: The county where an individual defendant resides has venue. The county where a company or corporation has a business office.

IOWA

Monetary limit: $5,000

General statute of limitations: Written contracts, 610 years; oral contracts, five years; personal injury, two years; and property damage, five years.

Time limit the judgment is valid: 10 years

Time limit for debtor to pay (or set up payment schedule): 14 days

State-mandated costs and fees: $50* minimum

Small claims court Web site: www.judicial.state.ia.us/Self_Help/ Civil_Law/Small_Claims

Information Web site: www.consumeraffairs.com/consumerism/ small_ia.html

www.iowabar.org/./d7ff6dc91c517cdb862567ba00690c91/
897d13fb9849b37a86256ee1005070cb!OpenDocument
http://public.findlaw.com/litigation_appeals/iowa-small-claims.html

Debt collection law: Iowa Code Annotated section 21-11-1-1 et seq.

Location within state of the Federal Small Claims Tax Court: Des Moines

Where to sue: The county where an individual defendant resides has venue. The county where a company or corporation has a business office.

*The fee structure in the state is complicated and expensive. Some of the clerks charge as much as $10 just to have a listing of the possible fees. Fees can be waived if the court thinks you cannot pay them, but if you win your case, the fees will be deducted from your judgment.

KANSAS

Monetary limit: $4,000

General statute of limitations: Written contracts, five years; oral contracts, three years; personal injury, two years; and property damage, two years.

Time limit the judgment is valid: 5 years

Time limit for debtor to pay (or set up payment schedule): Agreed upon by creditor and debtor

State-mandated costs and fees: $69 maximum

Small claims court Web site: www.kscourts.org/dstcts/smallclaims.htm

Information Web sites: www.consumeraffairs.com/consumerism/small_ks.html

www.ksbar.org/public/public_resources/pamphlets/small_claims_court.shtml
www.kscourts.org/dstcts/4claims.htm

Debt collection law: Kansas Statutes Annotated Section 15a-5-107.

Location within state of the Federal Small Claims Tax Court: Wichita

Where to sue: The county where an individual defendant resides has venue or where injury occurred. The county where a company or corporation has a business office.

KENTUCKY

Monetary limit: $1,500

General statute of limitations: Written contracts, 15 years; oral contracts, five years; personal injury, one year; and property damage, two years.

Time limit the judgment is valid: 15 years

Time limit for debtor to pay (or set up payment schedule): 10 days

State-mandated costs and fees: $25-$50

Small claims court Web site: courts.ky.gov/aoc/generalcounsel/faqsgeneralcounsel.htm

Information Web sites: http://research.lawyers.com/Kentucky/Kentucky-Small-Claims.html
http://law.freeadvice.com/resources/smallclaimscourts.htm
www.consumeraffairs.com/consumerism/small_ky.html

Debt collection law: Kentucky Revised Statutes, Chapter 24A.200-360.

Location within state of the Federal Small Claims Tax Court:
Louisville

Where to sue: The judicial district where an individual defendant resides has venue. The judicial district where a company or corporation has a business office.

LOUISIANA

Monetary limit: $3,000 ($2,000 in eviction cases)

General statute of limitations: Written contracts, ten years; oral contracts, ten years; personal injury, one year; and property damage, one year.

Time limit the judgment is valid: 10 years

Time limit for debtor to pay (or set up payment schedule): Agreed upon between creditor and debtor.

State-mandated costs and fees: $20*

Small claims court Web site: http://brgov.com/dept/citycourt

Information Web sites: www.small-claims-court.org/staterules.htm www.law.freeadvice.com/resources/smallclaimscourts.htm www.consumeraffairs.com/consumerism/small_la.html

Debt collection law: Louisiana Revised Statutes Annotated Section 9:3510 et seq.

Location within state of the Federal Small Claims Tax Court: New Orleans, Shreveport

Where to sue: The parish where an individual defendant resides has venue. The parish where a company or corporation has a business office.

*Varies from parish to parish. The small claims court Web site is one of the few that has returned to the Internet since Hurricane Katrina.

MAINE

Monetary limit: $4,500

General statute of limitations: Written contracts, six years; oral contracts, six years; personal injury, six years; and property damage, six years.

Time limit the judgment is valid: 20 years

Time limit for debtor to pay (or set up payment schedule): 30 days

State-mandated costs and fees: $50

Small claims court Web site: www.courts.state.me.us/maine_courts/ specialized/small_claims/index.shtml

Information Web sites: www.consumeraffairs.com/consumerism/ small_me.html www.research.lawyers.com/Maine/Maine-Small-Claims.html http://forms.lp.findlaw.com/states/mesc_1.html

Debt collection law: Maine Revised Statutes Annotated Title 32 section 11,001 et seq.; Title 9-A Section 1.101 et seq.

Location within state of the Federal Small Claims Tax Court: Portland

Where to sue: The district court area where an individual defendant resides or where a company or corporation has a business office has venue.

MARYLAND

Monetary limit: $5,000

General statute of limitations: Written contracts, three years; oral contracts, three years; personal injury, three years; and property damage, three years.

Time limit the judgment is valid: 13 years

Time limit for debtor to pay (or set up payment schedule): 30 days

State-mandated costs and fees: $20*

Small claims court Web site: www.courts.state.md.us/district/forms/civil/dccv001br.html

Information Web sites: www.peoples-law.org/misc/small-claims/small.htm
www.oag.state.md.us/Consumer/smallclaims.pdf
www.mdconsumers.org/II_ADVICE/h_smallclaims.htm

Debt collection law: Maryland Annotated Code Article 56 section 323 et seq.; Maryland Commercial Law Annotated Section 13-201 et seq.

Location within state of the Federal Small Claims Tax Court: Baltimore

Where to sue: The county where an individual defendant resides or where a company or corporation has a business office has venue.

*This is the minimum cost. Many cases will require five or more additional services of the court clerk at $5 to $25 each.

MASSACHUSETTS

Monetary limit: $2,000

General statute of limitations: Written contracts, six years; oral contracts, six years; personal injury, three years; and property damage, three years.

Time limit the judgment is valid: 20 years

Time limit for debtor to pay (or set up payment schedule): Varies with case

State-mandated costs and fees: $30-$40

Small claims court Web site: www.mass.gov/courts/courtsandjudges/courts/districtcourt/smallclaims.html

Information Web sites: www.lawlib.state.ma.us/small.html www.lawlib.state.ma.us/subject/about/smallclaims.html www.consumeraffairs.com/consumerism/small_ma.html

Debt collection law: Massachusetts General Law Annotated, Chapter 93 Section 24 et seq.; Section 49

Location within state of the Federal Small Claims Tax Court: Boston

Where to sue: The judicial district where an individual defendant resides has venue. The judicial district where a company or corporation has a business office.

MICHIGAN

Monetary limit: $3,000

General statute of limitations: Written contracts, six years; oral contracts, six years; personal injury, three years; and property damage, three years.

Time limit the judgment is valid: 10 years

Time limit for debtor to pay (or set up payment schedule): Varies for each case.

State-mandated costs and fees: $25-$65

Small claims court Web site: http://courts.michigan.gov/scao/selfhelp/smallclaims/sc_help.htm

Information Web sites: www.consumeraffairs.com/consumerism/small_mi.html

www.public.findlaw.com/litigation_appeals/michigan-small-claims.
html
www.learnaboutlaw.com/General/smallclaims/MI_small_claims.htm

Debt collection law: Michigan Complied Laws Annotated Section 19-655; Section 18.425

Location within state of the Federal Small Claims Tax Court: Detroit

Where to sue: The county where an individual defendant resides has venue. The county where a company or corporation has a business office.

MINNESOTA

Monetary limit: $7,500

General statute of limitations: Written contracts, six years; oral contracts, six years; personal injury, two years; and property damage, six years.

Time limit the judgment is valid: 10 years

Time limit for debtor to pay (or set up payment schedule): Varies for each case.

State-mandated costs and fees: $150* maximum

**Small claims court (conciliation court) Web site: www.mncourts.
gov/selfhelp/?page=313**

**Information Web sites: www.consumeraffairs.com/consumerism/
small_mn.html**
research.lawyers.com/Minnesota/Minnesota-Small-Claims.html
http://law.freeadvice.com/resources/smallclaimscourts.htm

Location within state of the Federal Small Claims Tax Court: St. Paul

Where to sue: The county where an individual defendant resides has venue. The county where a company or corporation has a business office.

*Fees charged vary by judicial district and may vary from this quoted fee average. Check with the court clerk of the district court for your county.

MISSISSIPPI

Monetary limit $3,500

General statute of limitations: Written contracts, six years; oral contracts, three years; personal injury, three years; and property damage, three years.

Time limit the judgment is valid: 7 years

Time limit for debtor to pay (or set up payment schedule): Agreed upon between creditor and debtor

State-mandated costs and fees: $30

Small claims court Web site: www.mssc.state.ms.us

Information Web sites: www.consumeraffairs.com/consumerism/small_ms.html
www.enotes.com/everyday-law-encyclopedia/small-claims-courts
http://public.findlaw.com/litigation_appeals/mississippi-small-claims.htm

Debt collection law: Mississippi Code Annotated Title 9, Ch. 11, Sections 9-27

Location within state of the Federal Small Claims Tax Court: Jackson, Biloxi

Where to sue: The county where an individual defendant resides has venue. The county where a company or corporation has a business office.

MISSOURI

Monetary limit: $3,000

General statute of limitations: Written contracts, five years; oral contracts, five years; personal injury, five years; and property damage, five years.

Time limit the judgment is valid: 10 years

Time limit for debtor to pay (or set up payment schedule): 10 days

State-mandated costs and fees: $25

Small claims court Web site: www.courts.mo.gov/page.asp?id=704

**Information Web sites: www.mobar.org/da48a652-2eaa-4adb-b9f0-ae0007b77912.aspx
www.rollanet.org/~bennett/bbsmclm.htm
http://law.freeadvice.com/resources/smallclaimscourts.htm**

Debt collection law: Missouri Annotated Statutes, Title 32, Ch. 482, Sections 300-365

Location within state of the Federal Small Claims Tax Court: Kansas City, St. Louis

Where to sue: The county where an individual defendant resides has venue. The county where a company or corporation has a business office.

MONTANA

Monetary limit: $3,000

General statute of limitations: Written contracts, eight years; oral contracts, five years; personal injury, three years; and property damage, two years.

Time limit the judgment is valid: 10 years

Time limit for debtor to pay (or set up payment schedule): 10 days

Montana state, city, or justice mandated costs and fees: $15-$20

Small claims court Web site: www.doj.mt.gov/consumer/consumer/smallclaimscourt.asp

Information Web sites: www.consumeraffairs.com/consumerism/small_mt.html
www.montanabar.org/displaycommon.cfm?an=1&subarticlenbr=32
www.uslegalforms.com/smallclaims

Debt collection law: Montana Code Annotated sections 25-35-501 to 25-35-807

Location within state of the Federal Small Claims Tax Court: Billings, Helena

Where to sue: The county where an individual defendant resides has venue. The county where a company or corporation has a business office.

NEBRASKA

Monetary limit: $2,700*

General statute of limitations: Written contracts, five years; oral contracts, four years; personal injury, four years; and property damage, four years.

Time limit the judgment is valid: 5 years

Time limit for debtor to pay (or set up payment schedule): Agreed between the creditor and debtor

State-mandated costs and fees: $24

Small claims court Web site: http://cdp3t0c1.cdp.state.ne.us/jcf

Information Web sites: www.supremecourt.ne.gov/small-claims/
index.shtml
www.unl.edu/asun/sls/handbook/court.shtml
www.enotes.com/everyday-law-encyclopedia/small-claims-courts

Debt collection law: Nebraska Revised Statutes Section 45-601 et seq.

Location within state of the Federal Small Claims Tax Court: Omaha

Where to sue: The county where an individual defendant resides has
venue. The county where a company or corporation has a business office.

*Will increase July 2010

NEVADA

Monetary limit: $5,000

General statute of limitations: Written contracts, six years; oral contracts,
four years; personal injury, two years; and property damage, three years.

Time limit the judgment is valid: 6 years

Time limit for debtor to pay (or set up payment schedule): None

State-mandated costs and fees: $46-86*

Small claims court Web site: www.clarkcountycourts.us

Information Web sites: www.consumeraffairs.com/consumerism/
small_nv.html
www.small-claims-court.org/staterules.htm
http://research.lawyers.com/Nevada/Nevada-Small-Claims.html

Debt collection law: Nevada Revised Statutes Section 649.005 et seq.

Location within state of the Federal Small Claims Tax Court: Las Vegas, Reno

Where to sue: The county where an individual defendant resides has venue. The county where a company or corporation has a business office.

*Fee varies on the value of the suit in dollars and with the county in which it is filed.

NEW HAMPSHIRE

Monetary limit: $5,000

General statute of limitations: Written contracts, three years; oral contracts, three years; personal injury, three years; and property damage, three years.

Time limit the judgment is valid: 20 years

Time limit for debtor to pay (or set up payment schedule): 30 days

State-mandated costs and fees: $72

Small claims court Web site: www.courts.state.nh.us/district/claims. htm

Information Web sites: http://doj.nh.gov/consumer/scc.html www.nolo.com/lawcenter/ency/article.cfm/objectID/ADF1FA1B-C67D-4B95-AD615532C3AE0862 http://research.lawyers.com/New-Hampshire/New-Hampshire-Small-Claims.html

Debt collection law: New Hampshire Revised Statutes Annotated Section 358-C:1 et seq.

Location within state of the Federal Small Claims Tax Court: None

Where to sue: The town or district where an individual defendant resides has venue. The district where a company or corporation has a business office.

NEW JERSEY

Monetary limit: $3,000 ($5,000 for claims relating to security deposits)

General statute of limitations: Written contracts, six years; oral contracts, six years; personal injury, two years; and property damage, six years.

Time limit the judgment is valid: 20 years

Time limit for debtor to pay (or set up payment schedule): 14 days

State-mandated costs and fees: $15 for one defendant; $2 for additional

Small claims court Web site: www.judiciary.state.nj.us/civil/civ-02.htm

Information Web sites: www.consumeraffairs.com/consumerism/small_nj.html
www.lawguru.com/faq/17.html
http://law.freeadvice.com/resources/smallclaimscourts.htm

Debt collection law: New Jersey Statutes Annotated Section 358-c et seq.

Location within state of the Federal Small Claims Tax Court: none

Where to sue: The county where an individual defendant resides has venue. The county where a company or corporation has a business office.

NEW MEXICO

Monetary limit: $10,000

General statute of limitations: Written contracts, six years; oral contracts, four years; personal injury, three years; and property damage, four years.

Time limit the judgment is valid: 20 years

Time limit for debtor to pay (or set up payment schedule): 10 days

State-mandated costs and fees: $120*

Small claims court Web site: www.nmcourts.com/sitemap.html

Information Web sites: www.consumeraffairs.com/consumerism/
small_nm.html
www.law.freeadvice.com/resources/smallclaimscourts.htm www.
articles.directorym.com/Small_Claims_Court_Information_New_
Mexico-r1145285-New_Mexico.html

Debt collection law: New Mexico statutes Annotated Section 646.005

Location within state of the Federal Small Claims Tax Court:
Albuquerque

Where to sue: The county where an individual defendant resides has
venue or where breach or injury occurred. The county where a company or
corporation has a business office.

*The fee varies from county to county.

NEW YORK

Monetary limit: $5,000; $3,000 in town and village courts

General statute of limitations: Written contracts, six years; oral contracts,
six years; personal injury, three years; and property damage, three years.

Time limit the judgment is valid: 20 years

Time limit for debtor to pay (or set up payment schedule): 15 days

State-mandated costs and fees: $15-$20*

Small claims court Web site: www.courts.state.ny.us/courts/nyc/ smallclaims/index.shtml

Information Web sites: www.tenant.net/Court/Howcourt/sclaim.html https://www.courts.state.ny.us/courts/nyc/smallclaims/pdfs/ smallclaims.pdf https://www.nycourts.gov/courts/nyc/smallclaims/procedural.shtm

Debt collection law: New York General Law Section 6600 et seq.

Location within state of the Federal Small Claims Tax Court: Albany, Buffalo, New York City, Syracuse, and Westbury

Where to sue: The political subdivision where an individual defendant resides has venue. The political subdivision where a company or corporation has a business office.

*For individuals filing a small claim; additional fees apply for appeals, demanding a jury, and commercial filings.

NORTH CAROLINA

Monetary limit: $5,000

General statute of limitations: Written contracts, three years; oral contracts, three years; personal injury, three years; and property damage, three years.

Time limit the judgment is valid: 10 years

Time limit for debtor to pay (or set up payment schedule): 14 days

State-mandated costs and fees: $90*

Small claims court Web site: www.nccourts.org/Courts/Trial/ SClaims/Default.asp

Information Web sites: www.aoc.state.nc.us/magistrate/small_claims.
htm
law.freeadvice.com/resources/smallclaimscourts.htm
www.legalaidnc.org/Public/Learn/publications/Small_Claims_Court/
default.aspx

Debt collection law: North Carolina General Statutes section 66-49.24
et seq; 75-50 et seq.

Location within state of the Federal Small Claims Tax Court:
Winston-Salem

Where to sue: The county where an individual defendant resides has venue.
The county where a company or corporation has a business office.

*Includes mandatory service fee.

NORTH DAKOTA

Monetary limit: $5,000

General statute of limitations: Written contracts, six years; oral contracts,
six years; personal injury, six years; and property damage, six years.

Time limit the judgment is valid: 10 years

Time limit for debtor to pay (or set up payment schedule): 10 days

State-mandated costs and fees: $10

Small claims court Web site: www.court.state.nd.us/court/forms/
small/forms.htm

Information Web sites: www.ag.state.nd.us/Brochures/SmallClaim.pdf
www.court.state.nd.us/court/forms/small/form7.pdf
http://law.freeadvice.com/resources/smallclaimscourts.htm

Debt collection law: North Dakota Cent. Code section 13-05-01 et seq.

Location within state of the Federal Small Claims Tax Court: Bismarck

Where to sue: The county where an individual defendant resides has venue. The county where a company or corporation has a business office.

OHIO

Monetary limit: $3,000

General statute of limitations: Written contracts, 15 years; oral contracts, six years; personal injury, two years; and property damage, two years.*

Time limit the judgment is valid: 10 years

Time limit for debtor to pay (or set up payment schedule): 14 days

State-mandated costs and fees: $15**

Small claims court Web site: www.ag.state.oh.us/citizen/pubs/ smallclaimscourtWEB.pdf

Information Web sites: www.consumeraffairs.com/consumerism/ small_oh.html
www.fcmcclerk.com
www.clevelandheightscourt.com/scguide.html
www.clelaw.lib.oh.us/Public/Misc/FAQs/Claims.HTML

Debt collection law: Ohio Revised Code Annotated Title 19, Ch. 1925, Sections 1-18

Location within state of the Federal Small Claims Tax Court: Cincinnati, Columbus, Cleveland

Where to sue: The county where an individual defendant resides has venue. The county where a company or corporation has a business office.

* No equitable relief. No jury trial. No discovery. No libel or slander cases. Right to sue may not be transferred. Court may order arbitration.

**Varies from case to case

OKLAHOMA

Monetary limit: $6,000

General statute of limitations: Written contracts, five years; oral contracts, three years; personal injury, two years; and property damage, two years.

Time limit the judgment is valid: 10-20 years

Time limit for debtor to pay (or set up payment schedule): Immediately or arranged between creditor and debtor

State-mandated costs and fees: $45-$147

Small claims court Web site: www.oklahomacounty.org/courtclerk/ SmallClaimsProceduresTxt.htm

Information Web sites: www.consumeraffairs.com/consumerism/ small_ok.html www.okbar.org/public/brochures/sccbroc.htm www.law-library.info/page/small-claims-court-by-state.htm research.lawyers.com/Oklahoma/Oklahoma-Small-Claims.html

Debt collection law: Oklahoma Statutes Annotated, Title 12, Ch. 36, Sections 1751-1773; Title 12, Ch. 5, Sections 131-141

Location within state of the Federal Small Claims Tax Court: Oklahoma City

Where to sue: The county where an individual defendant resides has venue. The county where a company or corporation has a business office.

OREGON

Monetary limit: $7,500

General statute of limitations: Written contracts, six years; oral contracts, six years; personal injury, ten years; and property damage, ten years.

Time limit the judgment is valid: 10 years

Time limit for debtor to pay (or set up payment schedule): Creditor's responsibility to collect debt

State-mandated costs and fees: $44.50-$88.50*

Small claims court Web site: www.ojd.state.or.us/mar/smallclaims.htm

Information Web sites: www.osbar.org/public/pamphlets/smallclaims.html
www.consumeraffairs.com/consumerism/small_or.html
http://research.lawyers.com/Oregon/Oregon-Small-Claims.html

Debt collection law: Oregon Annotated Statutes, Title 5, Ch. 46, Sections 405-570; Title 6, Ch. 55, Sections 011-140

Location within state of the Federal Small Claims Tax Court: Portland

Where to sue: The county where an individual defendant resides or "can be found" has venue. The county where a company or corporation has a business office.

*Depending on size of claim

PENNSYLVANIA

Monetary limit: $10,000

General statute of limitations: Written contracts, four years; oral contracts, four years; personal injury, two years; and property damage, two years.

Time limit the judgment is valid: 10 years

Time limit for debtor to pay (or set up payment schedule): 15 days

State-mandated costs and fees: $39.50-$65.50

Small claims court Web site: http://courts.phila.gov/pdf/brochures/ small-claims-court.pdf

Information Web sites: http://research.lawyers.com/Pennsylvania/ Pennsylvania-Small-Claims.html www.consumeraffairs.com/consumerism/small_pa.html http://law.freeadvice.com/resources/smallclaimscourts.htm

Debt collection law: Pennsylvania Statute, Title 73, Chapter 42-73, Section 2270.1

Location within state of the Federal Small Claims Tax Court: Philadelphia, Pittsburgh

Where to sue: The county where act occurred or individual defendant resides has venue or where breach of contract occurred. The county where a company or corporation has a business office.

RHODE ISLAND

Monetary limit: $2,500

General statute of limitations: Written contracts, ten years; oral contracts, ten years; personal injury, three years; and property damage, ten years.

Time limit the judgment is valid: 20 years

Time limit for debtor to pay (or set up payment schedule): Agreed upon between the creditor and debtor

State-mandated costs and fees: $30

Small claims court Web site: www.courts.state.ri.us/district/smallclaims.htm

Information Web sites: www.info.ri.gov/faq.php?ID=104
http://law.freeadvice.com/small_claims/small_claims
www.consumeraffairs.com/consumerism/small_ri.html

Location within state of the Federal Small Claims Tax Court: None

Where to sue: The county where an individual defendant resides has venue. The county where a company or corporation has a business office. If plaintiff is corporation, must be brought where defendant resides. If both plaintiff and defendant are nonresidents, suit may be brought in any county.

SOUTH CAROLINA

Monetary limit: $7,500*

General statute of limitations: Written contracts, three years; oral contracts, three years; personal injury, three years; and property damage, three years.

Time limit the judgment is valid: 10 years

Time limit for debtor to pay (or set up payment schedule): 30 days

State-mandated costs and fees: $80

Small claims court Web site: www.judicial.state.sc.us

Information Web sites: www.consumeraffairs.com/consumerism/
small_sc.html
www3.charlestoncounty.org/docs/Magistrates/summfaq.htm
www.law-library.info/page/small-claims-court-by-state.htm

Debt collection law: South Carolina Code Annotated Section 43-11-90

Where to sue: The district where either party resides or has a place
of business.

*No limit in landlord-tenant cases.

SOUTH DAKOTA

Monetary limit: $12,000

General statute of limitations: Written contracts, six years; oral contracts,
six years; personal injury, three years; and property damage, six years.

Time limit the judgment is valid: 20 years

Time limit for debtor to pay (or set up payment schedule):
Immediately, unless judge has provided time schedule.

State-mandated costs and fees: $17.98-$35.98*

Small claims court Web site: www.sdjudicial.com/index.asp?title=sma
llclaimsprocedures&category=public_info&nav=94

Information Web sites: www.consumeraffairs.com/consumerism/
small_sd.html#ixzz0M6GHKkXH

www.consumeraffairs.com/consumerism/small_sd.html
www.state.sd.us/state/judicial/court_proced/smallclaims.htm

www.research.lawyers.com/South-Dakota/South-Dakota-Small-Claims.html

Debt collection law: South Dakota Compiled Laws Annotated, Title 15, Ch. 39, Sections 45-78.

Location within state of the Federal Small Claims Tax Court: Aberdeen

Where to sue: The county where an individual defendant resides has venue. The county where a company or corporation has a business office.

*Fee includes postage for document delivery to parties.

TENNESSEE

Monetary limit: $15,000; in counties of more than 700,000 population, $25,000. (There is no limit in eviction or personal property suits)

General statute of limitations: Written contracts, six years; oral contracts, six years; personal injury, one year; and property damage, three years.

Time limit the judgment is valid: 10 years

Time limit for debtor to pay (or set up payment schedule): 10 days

State-mandated costs and fees: $71

Small claims court Web site: www.tncourts.gov

Information Web sites: www.consumeraffairs.com/consumerism/small_tn.html
http://public.findlaw.com/litigation_appeals/tennessee-small-claims.htm

Debt collection law: Tennessee Annotated Code Section 62-20-101 et seq.

Location within state of the Federal Small Claims Tax Court:
Knoxville, Memphis, Nashville

Where to sue: The district where any individual defendant resides, injury occurred, or transaction occurred has venue.

TEXAS

Monetary limit: $10,000

General statute of limitations: Written contracts, four years; oral contracts, four years; personal injury, two years; and property damage, two years.

Time limit the judgment is valid: 10 years

Time limit for debtor to pay (or set up payment schedule):
Immediately, or the judgment is enforced in justice court

State-mandated costs and fees: $62*

Small claims court Web site: www.texasbar.com/

Information Web sites: www.chiff.com/legal/small-claims.htm
www.peopleslawyer.net/smallclaims/texasstatute.html
www.texasbar.com/./ContentManagement/ContentDisplay.cfm
www.consumeraffairs.com/consumerism/small_tx.html

Debt collection law: Texas Statute, Finance Code, Title 5, Chapter 392

Location within state of the Federal Small Claims Tax Court: Dallas, El Paso, Houston, Lubbock, San Antonio

Where to sue: The precinct where an individual defendant resides has venue. The county where a company or corporation has a representative.

*Add $50 per defendant served.

UTAH

Monetary limit: $10,000

General statute of limitations: Written contracts, six years; oral contracts, four years; personal injury, four years; and property damage, three years.

Time limit the judgment is valid: 8 years

Time limit for debtor to pay (or set up payment schedule): 4 years*

State-mandated costs and fees: $60-$185**

Small claims court Web site: www.utcourts.gov/howto/smallclaims

Information Web sites: www.utahdisputeresolution.org/index.
php?page_ID=4
www.learnaboutlaw.com/General/smallclaims/UT_small_claims.htm
www.slcgov.com/courts/small_claims/small.htm

Debt collection law: Utah Annotated Code, Title 12, Chapter 1

Location within state of the Federal Small Claims Tax Court: Salt Lake City

Where to sue: The county where an individual defendant resides has venue. The county where a company or corporation has a business office or resident agent.

*Varies from case to case
**Depending on the size of the case in dollars.

VERMONT

Monetary limit: $5,000

General statute of limitations: Written contracts, six years; oral contracts, six years; personal injury, three years; and property damage, three years.

Time limit the judgment is valid: 8 years

Time limit for debtor to pay (or set up payment schedule): 30 days

State-mandated costs and fees: $50-$75*

Small claims court Web site: www.vermontjudiciary.org

Information Web sites: www.vtlawhelp.org/Home/PublicWeb/ Library/Index/1090200 http://ask.metafilter.com/83597/How-to-handle-a-landlord-forging- evidence-in-small-claims-court-VT www.uslegalforms.com/smallclaims

Debt collection law: Vermont Statutes Annotated Section 12-1-1 et seq.

Location within state of the Federal Small Claims Tax Court: Burlington

Where to sue: The county where either party resides or the event occurred has venue.

*Depending on size of claim in dollars.

VIRGINIA

Monetary limit: $5,000

General statute of limitations: Written contracts, five years; oral contracts, three years; personal injury, two years; and property damage, five years.

Time limit the judgment is valid: 20 years

Time limit for debtor to pay (or set up payment schedule): No limit

State-mandated costs and fees: Vary greatly and change frequently*

Small claims court Web site: www.courts.state.va.us

**Information Web sites: www.fairfaxcounty.gov/courts/gendist
http://forms.lp.findlaw.com/states/vasc_1.html6
www.small-claims-court.org/staterules.htm**

Debt collection law: Virginia Code Annotated Section 18.2 et seq.

Location within state of the Federal Small Claims Tax Court:
Richmond, Roanoke

Where to sue: The district where an individual defendant resides has
venue. The district where a company or corporation has a business office
or a registered agent.

*Garnishments, interrogatories, unlawful detainers, detinue seizures, levy
distress warrant, and writ of possession documents are each $25 more.

WASHINGTON

Monetary limit: $5,000

General statute of limitations: Written contracts, six years; oral
contracts, three years; personal injury, three years; and property damage,
three years.

Time limit the judgment is valid: 10 years

Time limit for debtor to pay (or set up payment schedule): 30 days

State-mandated costs and fees: $14-$29

Small claims court Web site: www.courts.wa.gov/newsinfo/resources/
?fa=newsinfo_jury.scc&altMenu=smal

Information Web sites: www.lawforwa.org/resources.html?iso1:
int=13&iso2:int=2970
www.tenantsunion.org/rights/22/guide-to-small-claims-court
www.consumeraffairs.com/consumerism/small_wa.html

Debt collection law: Revised Code of Washington, Title 19, Chapter 16

Location within state of the Federal Small Claims Tax Court:
Seattle, Spokane

Where to sue: The district where an individual defendant resides has
venue. The district where a company or corporation has a business office
or a registered agent.

WEST VIRGINIA

Monetary limit: $5,000

General statute of limitations: Written contracts, ten years; oral contracts,
five years; personal injury, two years; and property damage, two years.

Time limit the judgment is valid: 10 years

Time limit for debtor to pay (or set up payment schedule): 20 days

State-mandated costs and fees: $25-$45*

Small claims court Web site: www.state.wv.us/WVSCA/ProSe/FAQ.htm

Information Web sites: www.lawguru.com/faq/17.html
http://law.freeadvice.com/resources/smallclaimscourts.htm

Debt collection law: West Virginia Code, Chapter 47, Article 16 et seq.

Location within state of the Federal Small Claims Tax Court:
Charleston, Huntington

Where to sue: The county where an individual defendant resides has venue. The county where a company or corporation has a business office or a registered agent

*Varies from county to county.

WISCONSIN

Monetary limit: $5,000 (There is no limit in eviction suits)

General statute of limitations: Written contracts, six years; oral contracts, six years; personal injury, three years; and property damage, six years.

Time limit the judgment is valid: 20 years

Time limit for debtor to pay (or set up payment schedule): 15 days

Magistrate court costs and fees: $40-85*

Small claims court Web site: www.wicourts.gov/about/pubs/circuit/smallclaimsguide.htm

Information Web sites: www.consumeraffairs.com/consumerism/small_wi.html
http://law.freeadvice.com/resources/smallclaimscourts.htm
http://research.lawyers.com/Wisconsin/Wisconsin-Small-Claims.html
http://wilawlibrary.gov/topics/justice/civil/smallclaims.php

Debt collection law: Wisconsin Statutes Annotated, Ch. 799, Sections 01- 45

Location within state of the Federal Small Claims Tax Court:
Milwaukee

Where to sue: The county where an individual defendant resides has venue.
The county where a company or corporation has a business office.

*Depending on size of claim; changes frequently

WYOMING

Monetary limit: $5,000

General statute of limitations: Written contracts, ten years; oral contracts,
eight years; personal injury, four years; and property damage, four years.

Time limit the judgment is valid: 5 years

Time limit for debtor to pay (or set up payment schedule): 30 days

State-mandated costs and fees: $10

**Small claims court Web site: www.courts.state.wy.us/CourtRules_
Entities.aspx?RulesPage=SmallClaimsCases.xml**

**Information Web sites: www.consumeraffairs.com/consumerism/
small_wy.html
http://uwacadweb.uwyo.edu/studentatty/viewcat.asp?id=48
www.tetonwyo.org/jc/nav/100131.shtm**

Debt collection law: Wyoming Statutes Annotated Title 1, Ch. 21,
Sections 201-205

Location within state of the Federal Small Claims Tax Court: None

Where to sue: The county where an individual defendant resides has venue.
The county where a company or corporation has a business office.

US TAX COURT

Monetary limit: $50,000

State-mandated costs and fees: $60

Small claims court Web site: www.ustaxcourt.gov

Where to sue: See individual state listings in this Appendix.

NATIONWIDE PUBLIC RECORDS

KnowX, a LexisNexis® company: **www.knowx.com**

Public Record Center: **www.publicrecordcenter.com**

Public Record Finder: **www.publicrecordfinder.com**

APPENDIX C
USER GROUPS, NEWSGROUPS AND CHAT GROUPS

The following Internet newsgroups are available for users to ask questions of fellow members of the group. In the Google and Yahoo groups you ask a question and wait for someone to post an answer.

GOOGLE GROUPS

http://groups.google.com/group/smallclaimscourt?lnk=srg

http://groups.google.com/group/us.legal/topics?lnk=sg

http://groups.google.com/group/misc.legal/topics?lnk=sg

http://groups.google.com/group/alt.consumers.experiences/topics?lnk=sg

http://groups.google.com/group/misc.legal.moderated/topics?lnk=sg

http://groups.google.com/group/us.legal.self-represent/topics?lnk=sg

YAHOO GROUPS

http://groups.yahoo.com/group/courtcrusade/

http://groups.yahoo.com/group/sfgoodearthrealty/

http://groups.yahoo.com/group/unite-and-fight/

http://tv.groups.yahoo.com/group/powerofattorneylounge/

http://groups.yahoo.com/group/Judicialcollections/

http://finance.groups.yahoo.com/group/S_C_C_H/

http://groups.yahoo.com/group/court

http://finance.groups.yahoo.com/group/FightInsurers/

http://groups.yahoo.com/group/DCMACforum/

These newsgroups are more like messaging centers. If users are logged onto the group, they can ask a question and someone may answer back shortly. You can ask a follow-up question, and it will be answered as well. Although these are not necessarily a source of good legal information, you can trade experiences and ideas on how to solve particular problems. They are quite useful in getting answers.

USENET

Alt.lawyers

Misc.legal

Misc.legal.moderated

Us.legal.self-represent

Misc.legal.computing

OTHER:

www.thebostonchannel.com/news/13961147/detail.html

BIBLIOGRAPHY

Black's Law Dictionary, Fifth Edition, St. Paul, MN: West Publishing Company, 1979

Mastering Online Research: A Comprehensive Guide, Cincinnati, OH: Writer's Digest Books, Maura D. Shaw, 2007

Everybody's Guide to Small Claims Court, 11th Edition, Berkeley, CA: Nolo, Ralph Warner, 2006

Represent Yourself in Court — How to Prepare and Try a Winning Case. 6th Edition, Berkeley, CA: Nolo, Paul Bergman & Sara J. Berman-Barrett, 2008

Small Claims Court, Dobbs Ferry, NY, Oceana Publications, Inc., Margret C. Jasper, 2005

Small Claims Court : Step-by-Step, New York, NY: Barron's Educational Series. Inc., Ted Rothstein, D.D.S., 1997

The following Web pages were consulted in the development of this book (some Web sites may not be active upon publication of this book):

www.judicial.state.al.us

www.alacourt.gov

www.state.ak.us/courts/forms.htm#sc

www.state.ak.us/courts/forms/sc-100.pdf

www.supreme.state.az.us/Info/brochures/smclaims.htm

www.consumeraffairs.com/consumerism/small_az.html

research.Lawyers.com/Arizona/Arizona-Small-Claims.html

www.consumeraffairs.com/consumerism/small_al.html

www.alabamaLawyers.com/smclms.htm

courts.state.ar.us/documents/small_claims_info.pdf

www.arkbar.com/publications/pdf/scc_toc.pdf

www.consumeraffairs.com/consumerism/small_ar.html

www.districtcourtfortsmith.org/Civil%20Small%20Claims.htm

www.courtinfo.ca.gov/selfhelp/smallclaims

http://research.Lawyers.com/California/California-Small-Claims.html

www.smallclaimshelpline.com

www.kinseyLaw.com/freestuff/selfhelp/smallclaims/freesmallclaims
forms.html

www.courts.state.co.us/chs/court/forms/smallclaims/smallclaims.html

www.consumeraffairs.com/consumerism/small_co.html

http://research.Lawyers.com/Colorado/Colorado-Small-Claims.html

http://public.findlaw.com/litigation_appeals/colorado-small-claims.
html

www.jud.ct.gov/directory/directory/directions/smallclaims.htm

www.research.Lawyers.com/Connecticut/Connecticut-Small-Claims.
html

www.consumeraffairs.com/consumerism/small_ct.html

www.infoline.org/informationlibrary/Documents/Small%20Claims.

asp

http://courts.delaware.gov/How%20To/court%20
proceedings/?JPCourt.htm

www.consumeraffairs.com/consumerism/small_de.html

research.lawyers.com/Delaware/Delaware-Small-Claims.html

www.dccourts.gov/dccourts/superior/civil/small_claims.jsp

www.consumeraffairs.com/consumerism/small_dc.html

ann.sagepub.com/cgi/reprint/287/1/21?ck=nck

www.circuit8.org/sc

www.consumeraffairs.com/consumerism/small_fl.html

http://public.findlaw.com/litigation_appeals/florida-small-claims.
html

http://research.lawyers.com/Florida/Florida-Small-Claims.html

http://consumer.georgia.gov/00/article/0,2086,5426814_39039081_
39334516,00.html

www.consumeraffairs.com/consumerism/small_ga.html

http://law.freeadvice.com/resources/smallclaimscourts.htm

http://research.lawyers.com/Georgia/Georgia-Small-Claims.html

http://www.courts.state.hi.us/page_server/SelfHelp/SmallClaims/695

F88B9A961B33EAB295F3B7.html

www.consumeraffairs.com/consumerism/small_hi.html

http://research.lawyers.com/Hawaii/Hawaii-Small-Claims.html

http://en.wikipedia.org/wiki/Hawaii_State_Small_Claims_Court

www.isc.idaho.gov/material.htm

www.consumeraffairs.com/consumerism/small_id.html

http://research.lawyers.com/Idaho/Idaho-Small-Claims.html

www.ag.state.il.us/consumers/smlclaims.html

www.19thcircuitcourt.state.il.us/self-help/s_claims/index.htm

www.consumeraffairs.com/consumerism/small_il.html

www.law.siu.edu/selfhelp/info/court/smallclaims.pdf

www.judicial.state.ia.us/Self_Help/Civil_Law/Small_Claims

www.consumeraffairs.com/consumerism/small_ia.html

www.iowabar.org/./d7ff6dc91c517cdb862567ba00690c91/897d13fb
9849b37a86256ee1005070cb!OpenDocument

http://public.findlaw.com/litigation_appeals/iowa-small-claims.html

www.kscourts.org/dstcts/smallclaims.htm

www.consumeraffairs.com/consumerism/small_ks.html

www.ksbar.org/public/public_resources/pamphlets/small_claims_
court.shtml

www.kscourts.org/dstcts/4claims.htm

www.ktcourts.net

www.courts.ky.gov/aoc/generalcounsel/faqsgeneralcounsel.htm

http://research.lawyers.com/Kentucky/Kentucky-Small-Claims.html

www.consumeraffairs.com/consumerism/small_ky.html

http://brgov.com/dept/citycourt

www.small-claims-court.org/staterules.htm

www.consumeraffairs.com/consumerism/small_la.html

www.courts.state.me.us/mainecourts/smallclaims/index.html

www.consumeraffairs.com/consumerism/small_me.html

www.research.lawyers.com/Maine/Maine-Small-Claims.html

http://forms.lp.findlaw.com/states/mesc_1.html

www.courts.state.md.us/district/forms/civil/dccv01br.html

www.peoples-law.org/misc/small-claims/small.htm

www.oag.state.md.us/Consumer/smallclaims.pdf

www.mdconsumers.org/II_ADVICE/h_smallclaims.htm

www.mass.gov/courts/courtsandjudges/courts/districtcourt/
smallclaims.html

www.lawlib.state.ma.us/small.html

www.consumeraffairs.com/consumerism/small_ma.html

http://courts.michigan.gov/scao/selfhelp/smallclaims/sc_help.htm

www.consumeraffairs.com/consumerism/small_mi.html

http://public.findlaw.com/litigation_appeals/michigan-small-claims.
html

www.learnaboutlaw.com/General/smallclaims/MI_small_claims.htm

www.mncourts.gov/selfhelp/?page=313

www.consumeraffairs.com/consumerism/small_mn.html

research.lawyers.com/Minnesota/Minnesota-Small-Claims.html

www.mssc.state.ms.us

www.consumeraffairs.com/consumerism/small_ms.html

www.enotes.com/everyday-law-encyclopedia/small-claims-courts

http://public.findlaw.com/litigation_appeals/mississippi-small-
claims.htm

www.courts.mo.gov/page.asp?id=704

www.mobar.org/da48a652-2eaa-4adb-b9f0-ae0007b77912.aspx

www.rollanet.org/~bennett/bbsmclm.htm

www.doj.mt.gov/consumer/consumer/smallclaimscourt.asp

www.consumeraffairs.com/consumerism/small_mt.html

www.montanabar.org/displaycommon.cfm?an=1&subarticlenbr=32

http://cdp3t0c1.cdp.state.ne.us/jcf

www.supremecourt.ne.gov/small-claims/index.shtml

www.clarkcountycourts.us

www.consumeraffairs.com/consumerism/small_nv.html

http://research.lawyers.com/Nevada/Nevada-Small-Claims.html

www.nh.gov/judiciary/district/claims.htm

http://doj.nh.gov/consumer/scc.html

www.nolo.com/lawcenter/ency/article.cfm/objectID/ADF1FA1B-C67D-4B95-AD615532C3AE0862

http://research.lawyers.com/New-Hampshire/New-Hampshire-Small-Claims.html

www.judiciary.state.nj.us/civil/civ-02.htm

www.consumeraffairs.com/consumerism/small_nj.html

www.lawguru.com/faq/17.html

www.nmcourts.com/sitemap.html

www.consumeraffairs.com/consumerism/small_nm.html

www.courts.state.ny.us/courts/nyc/smallclaims/index.shtml

www.tenant.net/Court/Howcourt/sclaim.html

https://www.courts.state.ny.us/courts/nyc/smallclaims/pdfs/smallclaims.pdf

https://www.nycourts.gov/courts/nyc/smallclaims/procedural.shtm

www.nccourts.org/Courts/Trial/SClaims/Default.asp

www.aoc.state.nc.us/magistrate/small_claims.htm

www.legalaidnc.org/Public/Learn/publications/Small_Claims_Court/default.aspx

www.court.state.nd.us/court/forms/small/forms.htm

www.ag.state.nd.us/Brochures/SmallClaim.pdf

www.court.state.nd.us/court/forms/small/form7.pdf

www.ag.state.oh.us/citizen/pubs/smallclaimscourtWEB.pdf

www.fcmcclerk.com

www.clevelandheightscourt.com/scguide.html

www.oklahomacounty.org/courtclerk/SmallClaimsProceduresTxt.htm

www.consumeraffairs.com/consumerism/small_ok.html

www.okbar.org/public/brochures/sccbroc.htm

www.ojd.state.or.us/mar/smallclaims.htm

www.osbar.org/public/pamphlets/smallclaims.html

www.consumeraffairs.com/consumerism/small_or.html

http://research.lawyers.com/Oregon/Oregon-Small-Claims.html

http://courts.phila.gov/pdf/brochures/small-claims-court.pdf

http://research.lawyers.com/Pennsylvania/Pennsylvania-Small-Claims.html

www.consumeraffairs.com/consumerism/small_pa.html

www.courts.state.ri.us/district/smallclaims.htm

www.info.ri.gov/faq.php?ID=104

http://law.freeadvice.com/small_claims/small_claims

www.consumeraffairs.com/consumerism/small_ri.html

www.unl.edu/asun/sls/handbook/court.shtml

www.judicial.state.sc.us

www.consumeraffairs.com/consumerism/small_sc.html

www3.charlestoncounty.org/docs/Magistrates/summfaq.htm

www.sdjudicial.com/index.asp?title=smallclaimsprocedures&category
=public_info&nav=94

www.consumeraffairs.com/consumerism/small_sd.html

www.state.sd.us/state/judicial/court_proced/smallclaims.htm

http://research.lawyers.com/South-Dakota/South-Dakota-Small-
Claims.html

www.tba.org/LawBytes/T9_1800.html

www.consumeraffairs.com/consumerism/small_tn.html

http://public.findlaw.com/litigation_appeals/tennessee-small-claims.htm

www.tyla.org/pdfs/HowToSueInSmallClaims.pdf

www.peopleslawyer.net/smallclaims/texasstatute.html

www.texasbar.com/./ContentManagement/ContentDisplay.cfm

www.utcourts.gov/howto/smallclaims

www.utahdisputeresolution.org/index.php?page_id=4

www.learnaboutlaw.com/General/smallclaims/UT_small_claims.htm

www.slcgov.com/courts/small_claims/small.htm

www.vermontjudiciary.org/courts/superior/smclaims.htm

www.vtlawhelp.org/Home/PublicWeb/Library/Index/1090200

http://ask.metafilter.com/83597/How-to-handle-a-landlord-forging-evidence-in-small-claims-court-VT

www.courts.state.va.us/pamphlets/small_claims.html

www.fairfaxcounty.gov/courts/gendist

http://forms.lp.findlaw.com/states/vasc_1.html6

www.courts.wa.gov/newsinfo/resources/?fa=newsinfo_jury.scc&altMenu=smal

www.lawforwa.org/resources.html?iso1:int=13&iso2:int=2970

www.tenantsunion.org/rights/22/guide-to-small-claims-court

www.consumeraffairs.com/consumerism/small_wa.html

www.state.wv.us/WVSCA/ProSe/FAQ.htm

www.lawguru.com/faq/17.html

www.wicourts.gov/about/pubs/circuit/smallclaimsguide.htm

www.consumeraffairs.com/consumerism/small_wi.html

http://research.lawyers.com/Wisconsin/Wisconsin-Small-Claims.html

www.courts.state.wy.us/CourtRules_Entities.aspx?RulesPage=SmallClaimsCases.xml

www.consumeraffairs.com/consumerism/small_wy.html

http://uwacadweb.uwyo.edu/studentatty/viewcat.asp?id=48

www.tetonwyo.org/jc/nav/100131.shtm

www.knowx.com

www.publicrecordcenter.com

www.publicrecordfinder.com

Law.freeadvice.com/resources/smallclaimscourts.htm

www.lawyers.com

www.learnaboutlaw.com

www.odi.nhtsa.dot.gov

www.national-experts.com

www.consumeraffairs.com/consumerism/small_ak.html

touchngo.com/lglcntr/akstats/Statutes/Title22/Chapter15/

Section040.htm

www2.courtinfo.ca.gov/protem

www.ustaxcourt.gov

AUTHOR BIOGRAPHY

Charlie Mann

Charlie Mann, the author of *How to Win Your Case in Small Claims Court Without a Lawyer,* also wrote the novel *Polar Cap Five* and the fitness book *Built Hard* (with a foreword by World Heavyweight Champion Ken Norton). He resides in a rural area of Tennessee near the Great Smoky Mountains. He is a former instructor at the University of Tennessee and executive director of the public transportation agencies in Chattanooga, Tenn., and Louisville, Ky. He served as president of the software development firm CMA Micro Computer and as vice president of the consulting firm Voorhees-Generette & Associates.

INDEX

A

Abstract of judgment, 207, 203
Abuse of process, 207, 41
Accord, 207
Acknowledgement, 207, 201-204
Action of law, 207
Actionable, 207, 78
Actual damages, 207, 49
Adjudicate, 208
Adjudication, 208
Admissible evidence, 208
Admission, 208, 211, 165
Adversary system, 208
Adverse witness, 208
Affidavit, 208
Affirm, 208, 143, 52
Affirmative defense, 208
Allegation, 208, 210, 214, 21,
161-162
Allege, 208
Alternative dispute resolution
(ADR), 208
American Arbitration Association
(AAA), 208
Appeal, 209, 218, 229, 153-158,
189, 191-192, 38, 77, 101, 9
Appearance, 209, 221, 157, 60,
78, 93-96, 106, 111
Appellant, 209, 156, 192
Appellate court, 209
Appellee, 209
Arbitration, 208-209, 213, 256,
43, 61, 65, 113, 124, 16

Arbitrator, 209, 61
Asset, 209, 22, 170, 172, 180-181,
185, 193, 85
Assignee, 210, 197, 203
Attachment, 210, 182-183, 185-
187, 193, 95-96

B

Bad faith, 210, 47
Bank levy, 210
Breach of contract, 210, 212, 258,
28-33, 43, 63, 86
Burden of proof, 210

C

Calendar, 210, 150, 90
Capacity, 210, 216, 108
Caption, 210
Cause of action, 210
Chambers, 210, 120
Civil action, 210
Civil court, 211-212, 132, 136,
154-156, 158, 160-161, 173, 178,
180, 186, 192, 194, 35, 47, 49,
61, 63, 65
Civil law, 211, 238, 276, 44
Circumstantial evidence, 211
Claim of exemption, 211
Claim splitting, 211
Clean hands doctrine, 211, 72

Collateral, 211, 196
Collection, 210, 215, 218, 225-258, 260-268, 19, 23, 160-162, 164, 167, 169-170, 173, 175, 177, 180-181, 189, 191, 193, 199-200, 205, 33, 46-47, 50-51, 63, 10
Complaint, 211-212, 221, 229, 23, 37, 47-49, 101, 113-114, 122, 124
Confession of judgment, 211
Consequential damages, 211
Costs, 207, 209, 212, 214, 221, 225-269, 23, 132, 138, 140, 150, 153-154, 184, 186, 194, 28-32, 34-35, 37, 41, 44, 48-50, 52-54, 64-67, 69-72, 78, 98, 105, 114, 15, 6
Counterclaim, 209, 212, 50, 61, 113-114
Court, 207-223, 225-269, 272-276, 279-280, 283, 19-23, 131-133, 135-138, 140, 142-144, 149-165, 167, 169-173, 175, 177-189, 191-206, 25, 28-44, 46-55, 57, 59-67, 69-73, 75-83, 85-86, 89-96, 98-101, 103, 105-110, 112-113, 115, 117-119, 121-126, 128, 130, 15-17, 1-2, 5-8, 10, 14
Creditor, 212, 216, 226-227, 237, 239, 241, 246, 248, 256-257, 259, 149-150, 154, 160-164, 166-167, 169-170, 175, 178, 181-185, 187, 189, 194-196, 198-205, 95
Cross-claim, 212
Cross-examination, 212, 138, 148, 151, 102, 124, 126-128, 130, 8

D

Damages, 207, 211-212, 214-215, 218, 221, 228, 150, 154, 166, 184, 28, 30, 32, 39, 49, 53, 61, 70, 72,

74-75, 77-78, 80-81, 94, 102, 2
Default judgment, 212, 221, 143, 149, 60, 90
Defendant, 208-214, 217, 219-222, 225-259, 261-263, 265-268, 21-22, 143, 147, 155-156, 159, 169, 171-172, 177, 186, 188-189, 191-192, 194, 200, 202, 25, 32-33, 36-37, 39-52, 54-55, 57, 59-62, 66-68, 71, 74, 79, 83, 85-86, 89-93, 95, 98, 100-102, 105, 107-115, 119-120, 122-123, 126-127, 129-130, 16, 5-8, 10
Defense, 208, 213, 140, 40, 61-62, 102, 113, 123, 17
Demand for arbitration, 213
Deposition, 213, 132
Discovery, 213, 256, 132, 142, 149, 173, 69, 101, 114, 117-119, 126, 8
Docket, 213, 108

E

Enforce, 213, 223, 95, 115
Evidence, 208, 211, 213-215, 218, 222, 21, 137-139, 141-142, 147-149, 151, 157-158, 165, 25, 31, 36-37, 39-40, 50, 57, 61-63, 67, 71-72, 76, 82, 87, 91-92, 94-95, 98-103, 114, 117-118, 121, 123-126, 128-130, 16, 7-8
Execution of judgment, 213
Exempt assets, 214

F

Fraud, 214, 19, 70-71
Fraudulent conveyance, 214

G

Garnish, 214, 193
General damages, 214
Good cause, 214, 95
Grace period, 214, 160, 162, 164, 167, 77
Grantor, 215
Guaranty, 215
Guardian ad litem, 215, 81

H

Hearsay, 215
Homestead exemption, 215

I

Impound, 215
Inadmissible, 215, 142
Indemnification clause, 215
Indemnify, 215
Injunction, 216
Injury, 211-212, 214, 216, 225-268, 20, 144, 39, 54, 64, 95

J

Judgment creditor, 216, 149, 154, 160-164, 167, 169-170, 175, 178, 182-185, 187, 189, 194-196, 198-205, 95
Judgment debtor, 216, 142, 150, 154, 159-164, 166, 169, 171, 173-175, 177-182, 184-185, 187-189, 191, 193-197, 200-201, 203-204, 206
Judgment execution, 216
Judgment-proof, 216, 22, 177, 16,

L

Legal capacity, 216
Levy, 210, 217, 265
Liability, 217, 219, 19, 147, 165, 32, 44, 72, 111, 123, 15, 2
Lien, 217, 170, 193, 203, 33
Litigant, 216-217

M

Mechanic's lien, 217, 33
Motion, 217-218, 220, 137, 153-154, 179, 185, 188-189, 203, 94

N

Net income, 218, 53
Net worth, 218, 22, 53
Nominal damages, 218
Notary public, 208, 218, 192
Notation of appeal, 218

O

Objection, 218, 94

P

Per say, 218
Perjury, 208, 218, 161-163, 172, 198, 200, 205, 52, 96, 98, 107
Personal jurisdiction, 219
Personal service, 219, 109-110
Petitioner, 219
Plaintiff, 207, 209-214, 217, 219-222, 259, 21-22, 140, 143, 154-

156, 169, 177, 181, 186, 188-189, 192, 194, 200, 202, 32-33, 39, 45-49, 60-62, 67, 74, 80, 86, 89-93, 95-96, 108, 112-114, 119-120, 129-130
Pleadings, 219, 117
Pro tem judge, 219
Process, 207, 209, 214, 217, 219, 221, 23, 138, 140, 143, 152-153, 158, 169-170, 175, 183, 185, 187, 189, 191, 193, 200, 205-206, 31, 38, 41, 43, 48, 57, 75, 90, 97, 106-108, 110, 119, 121, 16
Process server, 219, 97, 106-108
Proof of service, 220, 60, 96

R

Reformation, 220
Release, 220, 166-167, 196, 203-204, 206, 105, 109
Relief, 220, 256, 49, 52, 69, 73
Repudiation, 220
Request for dismissal, 220
Rescission, 220
Respondent, 219-220, 156, 192
Response, 220, 133, 29-32, 40
Restitution, 221
Return date, 221-222

S

Satisfaction of judgment, 207, 221, 180, 196, 201-204, 51-52
Service by publication, 221
Service of process, 221
Small claims action, 214, 221
Statement of claim, 212, 221
Statute of limitations, 221, 225-268, 19, 43, 47, 55, 57, 61-62, 91,

113
Stay, 221
Stipulation or mediated agreement, 221
Subpoena, 222, 133, 139, 169, 171-173, 180, 185-187, 192-193, 196, 36, 41, 50-51, 65, 92-96, 100, 125
Substitute service, 222, 111
Summons, 222

T

Tangible property, 222
Tenancy at will, 222
Testimony, 212-213, 215, 218, 222, 21, 131-132, 135-139, 141-143, 148-149, 151, 63, 99, 102, 117-118, 124-129, 16, 8-9
Tort, 207, 212, 214, 222, 166

U

Usurious contract, 222

V

Venue, 223, 225-259, 261-268, 21, 37, 47, 55, 57, 59-60, 62, 90-91, 113, 16

W

Wage garnishment, 223, 227
Waive, 223
Writ of execution, 223